Dearest Jane &

May your days be grateful and
your hearts buoyant!

The
Grateful Jar
Project

Krystin Clark

Brightest Blessings,

♡ Krystin

Download your own printable jar template to fill with your own gratitude at www.krystinclark.ca

Krystin Clark can be reached at krystinclarkcreates@gmail.com

Published by Prominence Publishing www.prominencepublishing.com

ISBN: 978-1-988925-09-7

First Edition: October 2017

For Hazel

Table of Contents

Introduction:

I remember when I first encountered what would become my Grateful Jar. A turquoise glass canister perched upon a dusty thrift store shelf. It looked as though it may have been a holiday gift at one time. Maybe filled to the brim with bath salts or the like before gradually being used up. The empty container being cast off as a thrift store donation.

Originally I brought the beautiful jar home to hold the spare change retrieved from the depths of my pockets. Until years later I read about a Grateful Jar. The premise was simple: everyday for a year recording what we are grateful for. Over the course of the year filling a large jar with the notes. At year's end emptying the jar and celebrating a year's worth of gratitude.

What a sweet and soulful tradition, I mused! To pause amid holiday merry making; to sift, sort and wax nostalgic over a year of abundance.

Admittedly, a Grateful Jar was never my original idea. But I was intrigued enough by the experiment that I committed to partake in my own version. But instead of going from New Year's Day to New Year's Eve, I opted to initiate my Grateful Jar Project on December 21, 2015: Winter Solstice.

You may wonder, why start on Winter Solstice?

Winter Solstice is the darkest day of the year. At noon in the Northern Hemisphere the sun peaks at its lowest point on the horizon. It has the least amount of daylight and is dubbed the day with the longest night.

Our ancestors would have toiled tirelessly all year long to ensure they were prepared for the annual descent into darkness. Their survival depended on how well they had rationed their harvests. We don't have these pressures. Instead our preparations are more likely to be financial and psychological. To tighten our monthly budgets and prepare our bank accounts in anticipation for the consumer driven materialism of the modern age holiday season. To brace ourselves to face societal expectations and family obligations. To steel our nerves to march bravely onward through the drizzly grey of Winter and early Spring.

Ancients would have celebrated Winter Solstice as the imminent return of the Light. From this day forward each day is gradually extended in daylight hours. Amongst world religions, many of the December holidays are celebrations of the return (or the arrival) of the Light in one form or another.

I embarked upon the Grateful Jar Project to challenge my own perspective. To model an empowered mindset to My Little Roommates. Whatever I look for, I will find evidence to support. I saw my initiation of The Grateful Jar Project as my personal investment in the return of the Light.

The jar yielded a far greater reward holding my gratitude than it ever did in the painstaking accumulation of fifteen dollars in pocket change. Further what began as a daily ritual quickly became my floatation device in a year of swift dramatic change.

This is our story....

The
"Gratefuls"

December
2015

"THE PROJECT BEGINS"

December 21:

My daughters, herein referred to as My Little Roommates, have gone to the mainland to visit their father for the holidays. I don't refer to him as my ex-husband. Our words hold tremendous power. Perhaps that's why it's called *spelling*. I love the implication. The correlation between the building of words and casting spells. What I think, the emotions I feel, and the words I speak, directly create my day to day reality. So I choose to think good thoughts. Create good emotions. I choose to use the power of my words wisely. As Don Miguel Ruiz advises, "Be impeccable with your word. Speak with integrity".

I spent a good portion of my life with DaddyMan long ago. That ended and in turn, the chapter closed. He is the father of my children, he is: DaddyMan. Forever a pivotal figure in My Little Roommates lives. I am grateful they have him. Whenever possible, as much as possible, children need their fathers.

With My Little Roommates off on their Christmas journey, I am grateful for an afternoon of solitude. A roof over my head protecting me from the rainstorm, four walls sheltering me from a howling wind. Food in my belly and some time to paint today.

I cherish my alone time. I get the chance to remember myself. I don't get to hang out with her uninterrupted very often. Solitude is deep and powerful medicine for my Soul. I drink it up, like a dehydrated person stranded in the desert, cupping precious water, guzzling it deliriously.

Hello Beautiful Self! I remember you!! How delightful to bask in your presence again.

December 22:

Today at a friend's house I was caught in an uncomfortable situation between roommates bickering childishly. I felt physically ill from their exchange.

I am beginning to recognize red flags. Realizing that when I feel physically uncomfortable, *a boundary has been crossed*. The very moment it happens is when I need to take *immediate action* to rectify the situation. Not tomorrow. Not next week. I won't go home and think about how I will handle it next time. The time for the boundary is NOW.

As they bickered and gnattered at one another like children, one following the other to ensure the last word, I excused myself and left.

It felt wonderfully empowering. I am grateful to finally be learning the art of boundaries. This is going to be a game changer!

December 23:

The Wildling

Today this wildling
Spent longer scrambling
Up forested mountainside
Than she did last night
Curled asleep in her bed
Slightly less than full moon
Pouring moonlight through
Her window.
She sipped glacier mountain run off
Gratefully collected with cupped hands
From the rushing creek.
Climbed and cried in awe of the valley below.
Relieved herself in shaded corners of a mossy fairway
Rose staff and unleashed battle cry

Defending canine kin from the
Snarling lunging approach of another.
At home in silence,
She picks brambles from her hair
Empties pockets of heart shaped rocks.
Matches her vibration to unseen stars
And releases her intentions to manifest.
She bathes in candlelight, amongst bubbles
with her heart shaped rock friends
Scrubbing each clean
Kissing them and welcoming them home

December 24:

Curled up in the darkness, wrapped in a layered nest of bedding. I am stuffy and congested with a sore throat and chills.

I remember the first flu experience I had after leaving my marriage. Hunkered down in the bathroom, buckled hunching over the toilet. Vomiting. My three year old daughter happily riding on my back as if I were a horse. The realization that this was it: I was on my own and rather at their mercy in this moment.

Today I am particularly grateful for the opportunity to rest without having to concern myself for My Little Roommates. This doesn't happen often for independent parents. Words cannot describe in this moment *exactly* how grateful I am for the opportunity to rest and not be responsible for anyone or anything other than resting.

From my sideways view with my head resting upon my pillow, I savour a puddle of moonlight spilling across the hardwood floor.

My collection of crystals shimmering in the windowsill beneath December's Full Cold Moon. The night is alive with darkness and mystery. I am grateful to allow stillness to wash over me.

December 25:   **FULL COLD MOON**

Music pours forth from my speakers and I am grateful for ears and the gift of hearing.

Feeling moderately better after yesterday's dedication to deep rest, I dance alone in my kitchen. I dance to give thanks. To pay celebratory tribute to the Universal Mother Father Creator. I dance to raise my vibration. To hold joy in my mind, my heart, and deep within the fertile bowl of my womb. I dance to allow my Soul to savour great happiness.

After a day of hiking with my beautiful dog in the forest, my leg muscles give thanks for a different sort of movement. Surrounded by candlelight and crystals in the darkness, the full moon shines on the mountainside rental mobile home.

This is probably as good a time as any to announce: I am *all about* the moon. She is a fundamental cornerstone within my eclectic earth based spiritual practices. I am mindful to follow her rhythms, her waxing, her waning, her ebbs and flows as she hangs in the sky, looking down on us like an ancient mother. I set intentions on each New Moon when she hangs unseen in dark fullness.

Tonight as I dance and celebrate my day, every beat of my pulsating heart undulates gratitude. I am free. I am alive. There is stardust in the marrow of my bones and galaxies reflected in the depths of my eyes.

December 26:

I believe the Universe talks to us symbolically. Communicating through our surroundings. Through animals, synchronicities, numbers, and most powerfully, our Intuition.

Last summer I made a commitment to my Divine Higher Self, that I would heed all inspirations whispered to me. It wasn't a particularly graceful transition. Sometimes I would argue with it, then when I realized what I was doing, I'd laugh, shut up, and follow its lead. My Intuitive Life unfolded in many bumbling and fumbling stages.

Before we can embrace an Intuitive Life, we have to recognize the different ways our Intuition communicates with us. Learn its language.

Years and years ago, I stood with my very small children at a busy intersection on a major traffic artery in East Vancouver. Given the dawdling pace of the toddler at my side, I always waited to cross on a fresh traffic light. But one day, without explanation or knowing, I crossed on a stale green. There was no thought. No whisper. It was mere powerful spontaneous action, as though someone put their hand on the small of my back and guided me into action. I took my daughters by the hand, one on each side of me and we quickly crossed.

Halfway across the road the sound of disaster exploded behind us. The screech of burning brakes accompanied by the churning scream of twisting and contorting metal.

A semi tractor trailer had jumped the sidewalk. It had collided with the utility pole we had just been standing next to, and ripped it from its concrete roost in the sidewalk. The very utility pole that less than sixty seconds earlier, my youngest daughter had been happily and persistently depressing the pedestrian crossing button on.

Intuition isn't always dramatic bolts of deep knowing. More often than not it is the inexplicable phenomenon of tiny hairs standing upright on the back of our neck. That knotted feeling of apprehension in our stomach. Sometimes it can be a smell. Perhaps the subtle whispered message in the back of your mind. Maybe it is a magnetic attraction to a place, face or space. It can be something you just can't quite put your finger on.

It is worth the time and exploration to get to know your Intuition and learn how it gets your attention.

Intuition hasn't led me astray yet. Although, sometimes it has me raising my eyebrows in confusion as I am inclined to do something that, at the time, really makes no sense whatsoever. Yet when I heed Intuition's advice, it always works out in the end. If it's not alright, then clearly... it's not yet the end.

Tonight the Universe is being especially mischievous and particularly bold in her less than subtle communications. Opening a kitchen cupboard I found a red monopoly house perched front and centre on the shelf. This game piece was not here earlier. Of that I am certain. My Little Roommates have been gone for days, and I have been in and out of this cabinet throughout their absence.

I am grateful for the Universe's generosity of playful communication and this mysterious message. I am intrigued. Dear Universe: *Thank you for initiating dialogue. I will do my best to discern the mysterious message.*

I watch... *wondering*... waiting... I am willing. I am grateful.

December 27:

All day long I've been struggling with angstful churning of the Inner Critic and its pesky cohort: the organ grinding Monkey Mind.

Does your Inner Critic have a partner in crime? I imagine mine like a deranged organ grinder's monkey from days of old. It wears a little red and white striped shirt, and dons a tiny tasselled hat. Given its aggressive and unpredictable demeanour, sometimes I worry it may actually be rabid. It screams shrill monkey shrieks. It jumps about erratically making mischief and stirring up drama. It flings its excrement. Splattering it across the walls of my brain, soiling any sense of peace and tranquility.

Today, I have been navigating mental chaos.

It is time to pull out my soulful kaleidoscope of perspective. To twist and turn as I squint and search for the bright side. Twist and turn, twist and turn, twist and turn, *over and over again.* Exploring with profound curiosity and a great sense of wonder the shifting factors of today. Until, finally, Light shines through the ever shifting voids and I rediscover my gratitude.

Soaking in a bathtub tonight, I imagine green grinch like fingers reaching deep, deep down into my brain. Pinching to remove a writhing animated mind virus from a hole burrowed into the core of my brain. I whisper my tearful plea for assistance, *"Mother Father Creator, my 'Beloved I Am Presence', all my Angels, Ancestors and Spirit Guides, help me. Help lift this from my mind and shoulders. Please help relieve me of this.... It serves no beneficial purpose. Thank you. Thank you. I love you."*

I am grateful for a powerful sense of imagination. I am grateful for a team of unseen Lightworkers helping my healing and expansion. I trust I am learning new ways. I am grateful.

December 28:

I am grateful for the contrast between warm, cozy slippered feet and the cold floor beneath. Electric baseboard heaters can't combat the frigidity of vast emptiness beneath the raised mobile home. I am grateful for woolly layers, thick socks and a dog to snuggle with.

December 29:

Reunited with My Little Roommates today, they regale me with chatters of their feasts and celebrations with extended family.

Growing up I didn't have the opportunity to know extended family. The fact that my girls have a treasure trove of relatives makes my heart well up and skip a beat.

Today we are back together once again! We are happy, loved, fed, clothed and sheltered. All of our needs are met easily and abundantly.

December 30:

I caught a brief glimpse of My Little Roommates holding hands this afternoon while ice skating. On the car ride home, their voices filled the car as they sang along to John Lennon's 'Instant Karma'. *"We all shine on... like the moon and the stars and the sun...".* Tonight I watched them play glow in the dark Frisbee in the backyard. Twinkling stars and a meteor like Frisbee zooming between the two of them.

Sisterhood, love, happiness, friendship, song and laughter.

Thumpity thump thump
Thumpity thump thump
Beats my grateful, grateful heart.

December 31:

Universal Law of Oneness: We are all Beings emerged from One Energy Source. *We are all Beings emerged from One Energy Source.* This whole worldly EXISTENCE is Energy. The page you are about to turn is made up of Energy. Whatever you are sitting upon, is made of Energy. Everything you have in your refrigerator, is made up of Energy. Everything in your room, your home, your bank account.... all of it is a physical manifestation of Energy. Universal Law of

Vibration: *like Energy begets like Energy.* Imagine for a moment that every *word you speak* has an invisible length of fishing line emerging from you. Swung overhead with the great dramatic grace of a fly fisherman. Swooping, looping, bobbing and floating. Waiting, waiting, floating and waiting.... to hook into and return the catch to you.

Imagine for a moment, that every *emotion you feel* is a lasso. Swung overhead with the great dramatic ritual of a cowboy, swooping and looping, wrangling and snaring, capturing and returning a claim to you.

Imagine for a moment, that every *thought you hold* is an enormous magnet emitting powerful vibrations. It attracts far and wide, beyond borders and without limitation.

The majority of the population live in a reality currently dominated by fear based illusion. Many are consciously working towards shifting this. You are your own infinite Energy conductor. So. What are you emitting?

Are you using your powers for good?

Today I am grateful for an extended hike on my favourite patch of forest. My faithful canine companion and my beautiful blue eyed Little Roommate. Pausing so she could investigate discoveries with her new Polaroid camera. I smile knowing she is capturing memories with each snapshot.

Oh the healing therapeutic powers of immersing yourself in the forest. The breathtaking splendour of witnessing a young woman unfold in the discovery of herself. Be still, my beating heart.

January
2016

**"CHANGE IS COMING,
FOLLOWED BY GREAT SILENCE"**

January 1:

I am grateful for another beautiful hike in my favourite patch of forest today, this time with *both* My Little Roommates and dog.

There were BIG feelings, oceans of emotion, when one of them slipped on a frozen stream and smashed her iPod. Miracle of miracles, *somehow* the other Little Roommate and I managed to hold the space between ourselves and her emotional experience without being pulled into or bogged down by the extremes.

One of the toughest parts of parenthood is watching our children wrangle with hard lessons. Not stepping in to buffer, intervene or 'fix'. No one is served when we do that, and the potential lesson is lost. The next hardest thing for me as a mother, is to allow them to have their own emotional experience without it influencing my emotional state. I am learning to float atop their big feelings. You don't swim when clenching tightly, fighting the water. We float and glide when we learn to relax. So too it is with the emotions of our loved ones.

Life in our Ocean of Estrogen is always a bold adventure, never a boring moment. I remind myself this too shall pass. Until then, I breathe, and I trust. Twisting and turning my soulful kaleidoscope, searching, refocusing on my gratitude, Light beaming from betwixt and between the slices of experiences.

January 2:

I am grateful for the ability to wash laundry without leaving home. I wax nostalgic for a moment. Once upon a time, in my first year of independent parenting, being without a vehicle. Having to load a toddler and a mountain of soiled laundry into a stroller. Pushing it for blocks to the laundromat whilst the oldest was at school.

The clothes dryer here is broken. It spins but doesn't dry a single thing.

In this moment I could focus on disappointment that the dryer doesn't work. Or I can twist my soulful kaleidoscope and appreciate a large enough room to accommodate a rack of hanging wet laundry. Things here aren't perfect. But I opt to focus on what *is* working rather than what's not.

I am grateful for my physical, mental, emotional, and psychic health... and the privilege of doing laundry without leaving my home.

January 3:

Today I swept, vacuumed and mopped the kitchen and hallway floors. Taking the opportunity when I was finished to work with the energies of the waning fourth quarter moon. To sage the space. Banishing and releasing anything blocking the progression of my Highest Calling.

After months of contending with *ridiculously* outrageous electric bills, I am grateful to *finally* be on BC Hydro's twelve month equal payment plan. I am grateful for this freshly cleansed rental home; my family's nest, and knowing we will sleep safe and soundly tonight.

January 4:

I have been feeling great trepidation, cranky, even restless the last few days. Knowing from my own personal experiences, deep angst is often a precursor to a significant shift. With today being my day off, my biggest goal was to get onto the trail. To immerse myself in the soothing vibrations of the forest. To find solitary peace in the crunch of my footsteps. I wanted to savour what I call "the great shimmering defrost". An enchanted fleeting moment when the forest's Winter frost has begun to melt, but has not yet dripped. Hanging heavy clinging to the branch. Sparkling in its ripe wet fullness. Patiently waiting for gravity to do its thing.

Wait for it. I am about to martyr myself. Sacrificing my own needs and put my dog's happiness above my own!

We encounter a man and his eleven month old bouncy Labrador pup on the trail. Even though I had wanted solitude and silence, I felt compelled to join them on their walk. Rationalizing that it had been too long since Bella exuberantly frolicked, barked, and raised her shackles in a moment of play.

Their pace was faster than mine. So I upped my game to match them. I kept wishing the gallivanting dogs would settle down into a nice trot. She collides. Bouncing off a tree trunk. I realize she is so enthralled with her rough housing, she isn't paying attention to her surroundings. I am nervous about her on the ice. Yet I ignore this and we push forward.

We headed onto a new trail. While grateful for the guidance I hear a whisper from within *"these will be fun to scale back up"* as we scale down steep embankments. Ignoring the whisper, I persist and push through. I even tolerated indulging in small talk. Sigh.

We come across a roaring creek where my beloved dog quenches her thirst. Of course her beloved ball is caught in the current and washed away. She looks up at me with deep pleading eyes full of wonder and mourning. Yes, girl, welcome to consequence.

The rushing creek is too wide and too deep to be crossed by foot. I look down at his feet curious about his footwear. I wonder how he plans to cross? As though he reads my mind he shares, "there is a log over there I use to cross."

At this point my Intuition, which has merely been clearing its throat until now, has grown impatient. Resorting to elbowing me to get my attention, urging: this is the time. Part ways. Part ways!!

"Well" opting to respect my Intuition's urging instead of traversing a frosty log to cross a rushing creek, "I believe this is where we part ways".

"Can you find your way back?" he asks, slight concern in his voice.

Thinking of the steep hill I get to climb back up "Yes. I know the way."

Today I repeated a lifelong pattern: sacrificing my needs. While silent solitude had been my goal, I put that to the side and followed along on another's path.

I'm getting tired of this self sacrificing nonsense! At this point, my Inner Martyr is stomping about in my head wearing shoes two sizes too small. With great undulated pride she swings her flag of *look what I did out of the goodness of my heart for you.* Exasperated, I laugh. I see what I did but I took the means to correct it. I am learning.

Eat *that* Martyr... and put the flag of boastful sacrifice away.

I take a quiet moment to savour the majestic view as I scale back up the embankment. Out of necessity I find a sheltered corner of the forest to relieve my very full bladder. Dog sits at her end of the leash staring at me eye to eye. Baffled by the role reversal. "*Who is walking who now?*" I hear her playfully chiding in my head.

Before rising to pull up my pants, I hear a whirring sort of bird call overhead, looking up to discover five bald eagles circling above. Five. Isn't that interesting I muse to myself as I return to the trail. My morning tarot card was the five of wands today.

Note to self: When home, look up the meaning of five.

Change is in the air, and messages are all around me.

"Dear Universe: I am watching. I am listening. I am decoding. Thank you for your patience as I humble and stumble, spinning my decoder ring, trying to heed your message."

Finally back at the parked car, I lay my walking staff Gandalf into the trunk before settling Bella into the backseat. I'm still musing over the number five when I turn the key in the ignition Peter Schilling's song "Major Tom" pours out of the speakers, filling the cabin of the vehicle.

"The countdown's on: 4....3....2.....1, Earth below us, drifting, falling, floating weightless, calling, calling home...."

I laugh!! This is no synchronicity. The playful Universe is talking again, persistently ensuring I'm paying attention. Thank you. Thank you for making sure it didn't go unnoticed.

Having investigated, I learn that five represents change. It shows a jump between the physical and spiritual realms. The eagle itself represents messages of Spirit and creativity. Making positive choices and learning the lessons being presented.

Today I am grateful for messages. I am grateful I recognized I was martyring myself and took action to correct it. I am grateful that the moment I did, the Universe began speaking symbolically. Thank you. I love you.

January 5:

I'm grateful for last night's return of wildly vivid dreams as my body rested in deep slumber nestled amongst my favourite dark peacock blue bed sheets. I love those sheets. I love that colour.

January 6:

We woke to a significant accumulation of overnight snowfall. I am relieved we don't have to be anywhere, can stay at home warm and dry. I watch My Little Roommates and dog scampering playfully in the snow covered yard.

I am grateful for the childhood I have been able to provide for them. Their experiences are a direct result of changes I consciously made. Opportunities I bravely seized. I have done right by them. We haven't always lived in a rural environment, and I am grateful I was brave enough to take a giant leap of faith and relocate us from urban life years before.

January 7:

The store I work in part time is temporarily closed due to construction. I haven't had a stretch of time off in nearly three years. I am *beyond* grateful for the time to rest and relax.

The frozen lake across the highway from our home is slowly thawing. Magnificent slushy craters appear on its surface as it melts. I'm grateful Intuition warned me to be careful on an icy path. It was SO close, and I would have landed with a great hard thud.

January 8:

I participated today in an interactive online coaching workshop.

For several years now I've had yearnings as to what I *really want* to create in this lifetime. Last Autumn I finally committed to getting out of my way, and exploring what it would involve to make it so. I began working with a life strategist.

Myself, I am a trained Life Coach. I signed up for the training before I knew I was pregnant with my first born. I gave birth less than a week after graduation. My peers went on to do their practicums. Mine took a much different, much more long term commitment.

Sometimes we need the assistance of a professional to get things back onto track because, in the thick of it, we don't have the perspective. I consider these helping professionals equivalent to our side view mirrors on our car. They offer us an outlook that we may not have seen otherwise.

The extra beautiful synchronicity, is this life strategist was one of the first women I connected with after moving my family to the coast in 2013. A move that had been prompted by a disastrous catalyst: the near death experience of my youngest daughter. At age six she lapsed into a coma and was diagnosed with Type 1 Diabetes. An incurable, potentially life threatening disease. There is no cure, only life sustaining therapy in the form of multiple daily injections or being strapped 24/7 to an insulin pump. This is the epitome of my 'die, adjust, or migrate' attitude. We adjusted to what felt like life on Mars. Three years later we migrated.

Sometimes our darkest moments: the disasters, the illness or disease. These become our most empowering catalysts. The power is in how we *choose* to respond to it and what actions we take from there.

When I met this woman the first paving stone of our friendship was laid on a stretch of shoreline, accompanied by two exuberantly playful dogs. In an extra stroke of cosmic humour and irony, I had no idea what this new friend did for a living. Though I had been following her professional practice for some time on social media. I didn't know it was the same beautiful Soul from my morning walks with dog.

In today's workshop I'm being asked to contemplate some very profound questions such as *"how do I want to feel?"*. To then further consider *"when do I feel this way naturally?"*. Admittedly I am filled with delight at the opportunity to contemplate and daydream. But no matter how comfortable I feel with this woman. I am confused. Uncertain with how to proceed. How do you explain to someone that you feel the path of priestess calling you? It seems crazy. I'm not even certain what that would look like other than ritual and ceremony. People are going to think I'm nuts. I am so tired of being worried about what other people might think.

Today I am grateful for the opportunity to reflect upon my Life's path. To charter a new direction that truly resonates with my Soul,

To raise the sail of my beautiful ship and harness the winds of what is *truly* calling me.

Today I am grateful for permission to get out of my own way. To admit to those around me what I *really* want in this Life. I'm especially delighted at the timing of this course so I may harness the Energies of tomorrow's New Moon.

New Moons are the beginning of a new lunar cycle. Moons eventually became "months". It is said that New Moons are particularly potent astrological times to set intentions, to dream, and to set forth our plans to pursue our goals.

I am my own archeological dig and I am fabulously fascinated. This trek has some glorious treasure. I am incredibly excited by the possibilities.

January 9:   NEW MOON

Forty-three years of putting my desires on a shelf has me in a flat-lined existence of default. Yesterday's workshop has me recognizing how far off track my current reality is,

There is a yearnful longing deep inside my body. I think it's my Soul crying for my attention. It wants so much for me to reconnect with my purpose. To embrace my natural gifts and fulfill my Highest Calling. Right now my purpose seems jumbled. Tangled up and knotted inside out.

I believe I have a Spiritual mandate. A sacred contract if you will. My Soul agreed to specific circumstances in order to learn a particular curriculum. I further believe I will continue reincarnating to similar circumstances until I've demonstrated having this knowledge. I have learned some *very* tough lessons the hard way. Gems created by Soul splitting pressure. I'm not interested in repeating similar lifetimes because my learning plateaued and I failed to uphold the completion of my Soul's contract.

How am I going to get this back on track, how am I going to reclaim my Life?

The answer lights up in my mind in a sudden bolt of clarity: Kali-Ma.

Kali-Ma is the Hindu manifestation of the Divine Mother. The Goddess of destruction, rebirth and reincarnation. She is the ferocious warrior mother that smacks her children upside the head. Screaming at them to clean up their act. It's by no means a gentle love but a ferociously effective one. She is quite the fearful sight. Often depicted with blue skin. Hair spanning wildly about her face. Her protruding tongue dripping with blood. She wears a necklace of skulls from all of whom she has devoured.

Invoking Kali-Ma comes with the potential to destroy all of my personal illusions. Quite possibly annihilating all I have built thus far. But I rationalize that if I have built the wrong masterpiece, I am willing to invite her presence to wipe my slate clear. I am ferociously determined to get this Life of mine on track.

Beneath the dark sky of an invisible New Moon, kneeling in a room full of candlelight, incense hanging thick in the air I call her forth. In a hushed, barely audible ritual humbly requesting her Divine assistance. Whispering perhaps because of trepidation. I am nervous of what I am asking to occur. Giving deep thanks, I choose to hold the vision of all that no longer serves my Highest Good coming to an end.

May I have the courage to be brave and navigate the changes ahead with grace. I am grateful.

January 10:

The process of identifying self-imposed limitations has begun. Recognizing falsities my mind has convincingly presented as unswayable truths. I am grateful to be recognizing the many impacts of their distorted stories.

"Oh I couldn't do that" the Inner Martyr insists, "I have to work hard for my money". Continuing to bemoan "I don't have the time" "If I want something done right, I have to do it myself"

The Inner Artist jumps into the fray, "Artists can't make a living"
"I'm not talented enough"
"Who am I to dare do such a thing?"
"It has to be perfect"

The Inner Critic joins in: "I'm not smart enough"
The organ grinding Monkey Mind jumping into the fray
Flinging shit about....
"I'm no good at relationships."
"I'm not good enough"
"It's already been done."
"What you really want to do is bat crap crazy"

The Victim whines nasally, "I'm unworthy. I don't deserve it."

I remind myself, I am learning how to play a new musical instrument. An instrument I shall call my *true purpose*. If I insist on reinforcing how much I suck while learning I am probably going to end up quitting. *Whatever I look for I will find evidence to support.* I am learning to play a new instrument. This is brave and exciting! With time and practice it's going to sound beautiful. I'm beginning to examine and reprogram the stories rattling around in my brain. I will heal them, and I will change them. Actually: I am healing. I am changing.

No more "I will"... "I AM!!!"

I am consciously choosing to practice mindfulness. Observing my thoughts with deliberate detachment. By detachment, I mean I'm not taking my thoughts personally anymore. I'm no longer blindly accepting everything I think as truth.

When I hear stories parading into my awareness from my subconscious I will observe and without emotional attachment. I will say, *"Huh! Isn't that interesting"*

I'll watch with uninvested curiosity as they unpack their steamer trunks, flinging their beliefs around overhead. Then I will invite them to clear and clean. Purge what no longer serves. I will present new perspectives and I will back them up with supporting evidence. Then we will cooperate and repack our steamer trunks of truths. We ARE repacking our steamer trunks of truth. Together.

I am writing myself a new story.

Talking with a dear friend about stories, she suggests a voodoo doll for my pesky Inner Critic. I am grateful for the exchange of ideas shared between loved ones. My "Stop It Poppet" is being crafted. I am grateful for imagination and creative alliances. Grateful for the opportunity to play, sew and create. I'm grateful to be learning new ways. Grateful for my new *"Huh, isn't that interesting"* response. This is exciting!

January 12:

Observations in the forest: Bella does not question if she will catch the ball. For that matter, she does not question if the ball will even appear. She runs. Joyously. Exuberantly. Expectantly. Inherently doing what comes naturally: *intent on retrieving the ball.*

She doesn't worry about where the ball will land. She's not concerned if she will look silly or what the other dogs will think. She does not fear or fret. She is in the perfect vibration of absolute trust. She is absolutely aligned to her calling.

She leaps into the air catching the orange orb in her clenches. Hind legs reconnecting with the ground beneath her. Front paws landing a fraction of a second later. She radiates happiness.

At no time does she declare *"I can do that better, let me try that again"*.

Sometimes she misses by a fraction of an inch. The ball rebounding off her snout in a great arched neon flash into the woods. She does not mope that she did not catch the ball with her usual flair. She does not deem this as a failure, or any reflection of her whatsoever. It is what it is: a bounce in life.

She does not internalize the events. She is pure enthusiastic curiosity. Where could it be? A new adventure is afoot! The pursuit of the missing ball, hunting fervently and with great passion until she is reacquainted with it.

Occasionally the ball splashes into the creek. She will watch longingly as it is rushes away into the great unknown. She has not been abandoned. She has not been rejected. No one is out to sabotage her. There is always another ball in time.

As above, so below. This is the Universal Law of Correspondence. Do and Trust. With no exception.

I was reminiscing today about my beloved mentor, Hazel. I'm grateful for her many eclectic teachings, but what I'm most grateful for is the knowledge of Universal Law she instilled in me. Twelve years after her passing I miss her still. But I feel her with me. Sometimes I catch a glimpse of her from the corner of my eye. I'm grateful to have been loved and mentored by such a marvellous being of the Light. She was the absolute embodiment of unconditional peace and Love. May I honour your memory Hazel, in how I choose to implement and share your influence. Peace be with you my beloved Dear Wise Grandmother. Thank you. I love you. Thank you.

Today I'm grateful for observations in the forest. Universal truths embodied by dog, and the legacy of a Grandmother's teachings.

January 13:

I've recently recognized a behaviour of mine, a sort of self sabotage that I have playfully dubbed: hooked and rooked.

I get hooked. Snared. Pulled right up and away from my focus. But then like the rook in a chess game, I make a straight line in the opposite direction. All momentum stopped. Focus, gone. I have accepted the invitation of distraction. I have been: hooked and rooked.

This morning I had my day off blocked out. I knew what my top three priorities were, I had my desired emotions for the day. I had set my intentions! I was excited, full of hope, and ready to get down to some serious art making. All I wanted was to connect my iPod to my Bluetooth speaker and off I would go, productively, creatively and centred in gratitude.

But I couldn't for the life of me figure out where My Little Roommates left my speaker, and the longer I looked, the more frustrated I was becoming.

I looked high

I looked low

Messaged Little Roommates "where"

Only response "I don't know"

I got stompy

I started to fume

Muttering to myself as I searched each room.

For whatever reason I recognized the vibration I was emitting. This isn't the experience I want. This isn't how I want to feel. I had to let it go. Was a missing speaker worth hijacking my happiness for the day?

All I could influence in this moment was my inner dialogue. The thoughts I was holding that were influencing my emotional state. Rolling with the punches I returned myself to my desk refusing to get pulled into something I didn't want to experience.

Today I'm grateful for self-awareness and the ability to laugh at myself.

January 14:

The dark Goddess Kali-Ma didn't take long to grace me with her ferocious presence and swift change. Caught off guard I was knocked off kilter by a volatile and emotional blindside this afternoon.

It is becoming *crystal clear* to me that my time at my current place of employment is drawing to an end. I've felt this for the last year but I have a stubborn 'I can make this work' streak. A less than charming continuation of the lifelong pattern of sacrificing self for the benefit of another.

I am so scared to leap and leave my job. So scared.

"I call upon my Mother Father Creator, all my Spirit Guides, my Ancestors, and Elementals, please help relieve some of this emotional stress. Please help guide my reactions and responses for the Highest Good of All involved. Please help me to see what I do not yet understand".

Today I am grateful for my faith in an all compassionate Universe. Grateful for the lessons I am learning... even when they pinch. All I want is to handle this stressful situation with respect and grace. I remind myself this too shall pass and when it does, I will have earned and learned some amazingly powerful knowledge. Mysterious change is afoot and I am deeply grateful.

January 15:

The master bedroom of this house has glass French doors offering an expansive view into the backyard. Gazing out the window this morning I realized one single tree was absolutely inundated by a flapping swarm of dozens and *dozens* of chickadees. Not a single bird was evident in any of the other trees nearby. But this one buzzed with feathered activity. This peculiar sight was undoubtedly another playful message from the Universe.

I am grateful for this happy community of chickadees singing their *"chick-a-dee-dee-dee"* call. The symbolism of this animal reminding me I am bringing forth new growth into my Life. Big messages from a tiny bird. I'm grateful for the sight, the sung message, and my curiosity to investigate it. Animal medicine is another gift bestowed by my beloved Hazel. She planted some powerful seeds in my Life before parting. I am so grateful for the privilege of carrying her wisdoms. I am becoming a woman beyond anything I ever could have dared dream or imagine.

January 16:

After the weird and strained encounter the other day at work I am grateful to have received an email from my employer on my day off. Technology has allowed both of us to pause and process before communicating. I feel solidly grounded in my truth. This situation is reenacting patterns that no longer serve.

I call yet again on my 'Beloved I Am Presence', upon Mother Father Creator and on all of my Lightworking team to assist me in responding diplomatically for the Highest Good of All involved.

Today I am grateful for technology, communication and clarity. Grateful for my team of Lightworkers. Weirdness is afoot. But I've got my trusty soulful kaleidoscope, and I'm going to keep on twisting and turning until I have refocused on gratitude.

January 17:

> I am grateful for the sky
> I am grateful for the moon
> I am grateful for my daughters
> Sleeping peacefully in the next room.

Recording my gratitude in this strange time of uncertainty brings me great comfort. I suppose I am grateful for the power of gratitude. I ask for assistance to be patient. Support in holding a trusting heart.

Whatever is unfolding... it's big!

I can feel it in my bones.

January 18:

It is time to get out of my own way and move onto new adventures! I am grateful for all the validating signs and messages from the Universe over the past week. I have decided to give five weeks notice to allow time to hire and train my replacement. I am not interested in a great dramatic upheaval within the store and would rather a gradual exit, ensuring my employer is not left in a lurch. My final day will be March 15th. I am grateful for clarity. Adventure is afoot and opportunity is in the air!

<u>January 19:</u>

I submitted my resignation this afternoon. I was abruptly told to leave now. I never anticipated this response! It wasn't even a blip on my Intuitive radar. I had a decade-old moment of reflection involving a similar circumstance. In my tenacious twenties I had a conflict with an older female supervisor I had worked under for five years. During which time I took everything personally and stuffed all my anger and resentments from our interactions. Until one day I lost my cool and I exploded like a volcano. In the middle of the office I cussed her out and stormed out in a rage never to return again.

This time I did it so very differently. Today I celebrate how far I have come in my personal growth. I was respectful and diplomatic even while setting clear boundaries. I wasn't reactive, impulsive or rude. I changed my role in this interpersonal dynamic. I am grateful that this very unanticipated last day was indeed an awesome one full of synchronicities. I felt light, free and happy. Proud of a job well done. The shop filled with brilliant soft sunshine, and all the right people came in through the door one at a time as though I had beckoned them.

I whispered to one of them as I hugged her, "I've been calling you in my mind for days!"

She smiled and replied, "I only heard it yesterday."

I am profoundly grateful this has been part of my experience for the last three years. Though I am terrified. Shaking with exhilaration of the vast unknown. I feel like a meteor bursting through the night sky. I very deliberately choose to hold tight to gratitude. *There is no benefit in focusing on anything else.* What I think, I create. Whatever I focus on, I feed and amplify. This is a powerful moment of co-creating. If I focus on stress and uncertainty, I generate more stress and uncertainty. I focus on gratitude, more circumstances to be grateful will appear.

I give thanks to dark Goddess Kali-Ma for her efforts thus far and immediate dramatic shifts.

The pressure of sudden unexpected change brought forth a heart-felt poem written as I soaked sobbing in the bathtub. I bob in a sea of uncertainty clenching the only floatation device I have at my disposal: gratitude.

The only way out Is Through

I used to know a red room
warm, comforting, nourishing
Calling me to grow into something more.

There was safety in that space
Hushed voices, white noise.
The mysterious metronome of a heartbeat.

I outgrew my cozy nest. Cramped and stuck
Longing for the freedom to stretch beyond.
Change came along one day
Suddenly, with little warning.
Or... perhaps I was too cramped to sense it?

The walls closed in, my head
Throbbing. My face, pulsating
The whooshing of my heartbeat in my ears.

Tingling from head to toe
Visibly shaking
Uncertain of the vast unknown awaiting.

No way out but through
Oh the pressure-
No way out but through. Surrender. Flow.
Change bore down on me
Fast and furious today
The world pressing down.

I think of that red room. Walls closing in
Strange, isn't it?
The parallel sensations
Between terror and excitement.

My heart whooshes again in my ears
The only way out is through. Oh the pressure-
You are being pushed. Do not resist.
Surging pressure
Surrender...
This is rebirth
And the only way out
Is through.

Today I am grateful for new opportunities. Synchronistic encounters. Deep soaker bathtubs, the cathartic release of tears and the expression of poetry.

January 20:

"Go silent" Intuition began whispering to me last night in the bathtub. I resisted. But it is being stubbornly persistent. *"Go silent. Be still. Take your time. How you handle this shows who you really are."*

Last summer I committed to myself, and to Spirit, that I would heed all that my Intuition instructed of me. It all started with a prompting to initiate 30 Grateful Selfies on Instagram. Selfless plug you can check them out with the hashtag #30gratefulselfies. It culminated with me doing a song and dance on FaceBook. I am not a song and dance type person. I naively thought I'd proven to Intuition and Spirit I would do everything uncomfortable I ever thought I'd be called to do. Looking back now, I laugh at the adorable naivete that I thought a song and dance on social media would be the most awkward and uncomfortable thing I was prompted to do.

There is no half in half out on a commitment like that. I cannot in good faith, tell my Highest Self that I will heed all Intuitive instructions only to argue, *"Yeah, not that one. That's too big"*.

This morning I pulled the Hermit tarot card. The shrouded figure, head hung in its garbed cloak, holding a lantern. Hermits probably don't talk. Alright, Intuition. Alright. I hear you. I will follow your lead. Tomorrow I embark on a seven-day voice vacation.

Dear Intuition: While I say I will follow your lead, it doesn't mean I'm excited or joyful at the prospect. But I will do my best not to grumble or kick my feet in protest the whole way along. Not so much as a gesture for you. But because I recognize that's one more way I make things harder for myself. Wait. I stand corrected. That is just one more way I USED to make things harder for myself. I forgot. I'm letting *that* go.

Normally the logistics of silence wouldn't have worked. But suddenly, and most serendipitously, I have all the time in the world and no place to be. I don't understand the instruction but I can feel it in my bones: there is something for me to learn in a journey of quiet processing.

In a perfect situation I'd visit an ashram in the mountains to embark on such contemplation. But the logistics of that would be far more complicated. Further I don't need external means to go within. I am already in the mountains. I am my own guru. So I establish parameters of this experience: Life will go on for myself and My Little Roommates. I will continue to be an active participant. I will continue to meet all of their needs that I am responsible for; there will be no neglect. I will simply be doing it without using my voice. I can, and will, communicate with others around me. Just not vocally. Seems doable, right?

Should I be concerned, somewhere in the depths, I hear laughter echoing in my head?

My Little Roommates are not impressed. In fact, they are as angry as a swarm of bees whose hive has been poked and prodded. While I have compassion for their responses, this is non-negotiable. There is some sort of deep buried treasure here for me. My instruction will not be thwarted for the emotional comfort of another. My learning will not stagnate to accommodate their preferences. Perhaps there are lessons in this for them as well. Maybe they will learn how to hold the space for the actions of others not to disrupt their own peace. Maybe I am delusional in that hope. Time will tell.

Tonight, I am grateful for the whispers of Intuition. Stubborn whispers that refuse to be ignored. I am grateful for mysterious opportunities to seize strange adventures. Deep thanks for all the lessons that are appearing before me.

Thank you Intuition. Thank you being one of the frequencies of my communications with the Universe. I am listening. I am willing. I am game. Let's do this!

<u>January 21:</u>   **DAY ONE OF FULL SILENCE**

My invocation of the dark Goddess Kali-Ma has washed what I perceived to be stable ground out from beneath my feet. Crashing out from under me like the tumbled churning of a roaring mudslide. I scramble. Reeling with shock.

It's important to me that I do no harm in my discombobulated state. Hurt people hurt people. I don't want to launch into reactiveness like a fallen electrical wire spewing a spray of burning sparks. My Little Roommates will not bear the verbal sting of my emotional reeling. I will do no harm. Therefore, I need the opportunity to pause. To do an internal autopsy of what transpired so I do not repeat this dynamic again.

In my first full day of silence, I heard a lot of "I miss you". Which I found interesting, given that am making a conscious effort to be more present in other ways. Deep eye contact. Exaggerated body language. Affection. Hugs. Yet still, "I miss you". I am quickly uncovering how much voice is associated with presence. Not just for ourselves but for those around us.

I am also very quickly learning how much my Energy I leak trying to be funny. Wanting to make everyone laugh. Wanting everyone to be happy.

I am also recognizing how ineffectively I use words to express myself. Flapping my lips about trying to help. Trying to fix, trying to uplift, trying to encourage, trying to organize. How often words tumble off my lips to fill silence. Ironic how tossing words into a void only expands that void. The only thing that can fill the void is heartfelt intention. I'm realizing how rarely connected I am. Silence is allowing the non-negotiable space for my mourning to dissipate.

Know what happens when you take away your external voice? You come up close and personal with your internal dialogue. It can no longer be avoided. My Inner Critic wants to play a spiked game of dodgeball. Her diabolical organ grinding Monkey Mind jumping up and down yelping great dark twisted shrieks of excitement.

Since my stories are very quickly stepping forward with their baggage, I'm better able to recognize judgements and derogatory opinions as they appear. Since I'm not voicing them my Energy has been turned inward to explore with curiosity. Inquiring: *"What judgement am I experiencing about this person? How is this judgement really about me?"*

When I ask myself, *"What evidence do I have that supports this judgement?"* This is where distorted stories begin crumbling. Presenting the opportunity to replace it with an empowered belief.

One of the most profound stories that presented nearly immediately is one that has kept me mummified. I have observed I am not comfortable with women. Recognizing that until recently (see- I'm already beginning to shift it with the power of language) in my female friendships I have always kept one foot out the door. Prepared to turn and bolt.

Women tend to scare me. Wait: rewrite!! Women *used* to scare me. I *used* to view them as unpredictable. Dramatic. Volatile. Turbulent mood swings. Catty. Gossip. Backstabbing. Treachery. Betrayal. Even violent. I have exhibited these behaviours myself. As much as I admire the philosophy of women helping women I haven't always witnessed it.

Like Energy attracts like Energy. Universal Law of Vibration. As long as fear of toxic possibilities lay *anywhere* in my belief system, I emit vibrations of that story. Thereby attracting the experience. Essentially recreating it.

Dear Self....Dear World: I am so sorry such an entrenched twisted perspective skewed my reality. Limiting my experience of community. I am putting this story down. Walking away without it. Before I used to drop it only to pick it right back up (I'm working on that). Like a piece of molten rock it burns my hands. Bleeding, everything I touch is coloured by the wound.

I forgive myself. Forgive all of this. I will no longer subconsciously anticipate this experience. What I see in you is a reflection of myself. I offer us both Love because we are not separate. We are One. For me to judge one I judge all. I get that now.

Wow. I am doing a lot of *"Huh, isn't that interesting"* in this silent experiment thus far.

I am also sending out a lot of Love. To everyone. Everywhere. Myself included. A lot of Love. May we all have the courage to heal what we need to heal so we may step into what we are being called to be. Myself included.

Dear Universe: please help me heal this. I have work to do and I can't do it clutching a cape of warped stories.

I am grateful for the splitting explosion of my seed. For the turbulence of new growth. For all that is being shed and released. I am grateful for deep powerful shifts found in the silence.

Thank you, dark mother, Kali-Ma. I am so grateful. I will breathe. I will be brave. I'm learning new ways and writing a new story.

I am grateful.

Communicating with my children has been a bit of an adventure. Dog is downright confused; I think I forgot to give her my "going into silence" preparatory speech. I'll have to write the girls a note to fill her in. I have realized in my silence how often I simply speak as a reflex. It is much harder to be critical of others when you're not speaking. It is also much harder to be pulled into drama or arguments. I found that an especially interesting observation. At first, my kids thought I was angry and giving them the silent treatment. I was surprised by that. So I played with my body language more. It became a bit of a game, dramatic charades in the kitchen. Many hugs. Much stroking of hair. A lot of gazing deeply into their eyes, a warm smile on my face, nothing but Love in my heart.

It has also been interesting to observe over the last couple of days how much more grounded and centred I have been feeling. More mindful of my body language. More creative and expressive. More engaged. Strangely.... more tolerant.

I am coming to witness how often people assume how others are feeling and how inaccurate those assumptions are. I am realizing how words cannot quell another's big emotions. But a silent mouth somehow holds the space for another's expression, whether verbal or in the form of tears, and that.... that is where the shift in our emotional experience begins. Being heard. Being understood. I wish I could bottle the insights that I am realizing. So that when I return to the land of the speaking I can ask myself: Am I trying to fill the vacuum? Am I speaking to eliminate awkwardness? Are my words only making the situation more uncomfortable? *Is it my intention to understand the person speaking to me?*

I am surprised to discover a mysterious peace that accompanies silence. Far more than I ever anticipated experiencing.

January 23: **DAY THREE OF SILENCE**
FULL WOLF MOON

Days are slowly beginning to stretch slightly longer. I gratefully note the sun setting at 5:10pm. Midwinter will soon be here. I am grateful for freshly washed sheets hanging on the clothesline overnight. They will not dry there. I have no expectations of them doing so. They are there to bask in the full moon light. To infuse my future dreams with moon beams.

There has been some emotional static tonight. In a moment of particularly heavy tension, one of My Little Roommates passes me a yellow square of paper. She has written the headline "5 Greatfulls" and on that slip of paper, has drawn lines, each numbered 1-5, for me to identify my five "gratefuls" for the night.

For the first time the ripple effect of The Grateful Jar Project is becoming evident. My gratitude appears in the form of tears filling my eyes and slowly trickling down my cheeks.

January 24: **DAY FOUR OF SILENCE**

I avoided it as long as I possibly could. But the time has come: I have to venture into town. I am afraid of being judged. Of being deemed crazy or eccentric. Then I realized *"who do I really think I am fooling? I am eccentric. Maybe even crazy, what's the big deal? Why am I trying to present as something that I am not?"* I am unsettled by how much concern I place on what others think of me. When what I want more than anything is the freedom to be myself. What would happen if I stopped concerning myself about the regard of others? Yes. That would be freedom. Interesting! One more way how I make this harder on myself. If I release the concern, I have embraced freedom. *Isn't that interesting!*

I made a little note and pinned it onto my sweater before leaving the house. After all, I didn't want people to think I was just being rude and ignoring them. Aaaah yes, look at that people pleasing streak again *"Please don't think I'm rude. Please don't take this personally."* Please.... Please.... Please.... Oh the pleas of the people pleaser.

The list of places I have to go to is rather substantial, and I am still feeling very nervous. So I opt to go to the library first, thinking that my silence would be appreciated, or at the very least, barely noticed there. Sure, barely noticed. You are wearing a note calling attention to it. I am an enigma wrapped in a paradox.

The library was uneventful and I had a bit of confidence under my belt. This was totally doable!

Venturing into the next store, I take my purchase to the counter and the cashier says to me, ""Oh my GOSH do I understand what YOU are doing". Her intensity surprised me, caught me off guard for a moment. How is it that I hadn't even *considered* I'd find a like-minded person that understood my endeavour? Instead I had focused on being misunderstood. The Inner Critic and her Monkey Mind cohort are playing head games with me in a tag team effort, manipulating my belief system through isolation. Separateness. Convincing me that I am so far out there, no one would be able to relate, or understand where I am coming from. *Isn't that interesting.*

"What you're doing takes a lot of strength," the cashier says to me warmly. "I am really proud of you". This catches me off guard big time! My mouth quivered, my eyes welled, I bowed my head in thanksgiving, and then I bolted to the door before tears flowed down my cheeks. I had just been seen. I had just been understood.

Grocery store. I went through a young man's check stand who never seemed to want to chit chat. I thought that would be a good fit. I suppose he was intrigued by the small sign on my sweater, as was the cashier behind him.

"What does your sign say?" she squawked her curiosity from two checkstands over. Coming around to read aloud, "I am in silence, thank you for your understanding".

"Wow! Are you sick?" she asked, worried. I make the whirling crazy gesture beside my head. She laughs. "Wow". She said again, "What do you do if it's an emergency and you have to talk?" I pull a note pad out of my pocket and untuck the pen behind my ear smiling. "I could never do that!! You sure are strong".

In this very moment of writing these two exchanges, I struggle, feeling boastful sharing the comments I'm strong. *Isn't that interesting.* We are so insistent in our efforts to resist compliments. Dismissing comments about our strength. Accept. Receive. Appreciate. We are strong. Stronger than we ever realize. Let's lay down the shields of deflection. Let's let the good stuff in.

January 25:   **DAY FIVE OF SILENCE**

One of My Little Roommates scrambles onto my bed as I journal. She curls up into my lap, big eyes prompting "love me". I fold her, without words, into my wings. Cuddling with her until the sounds of our breath synchronize and we sound like a purring cat. So crazy grateful.

At bedtime I hold one of them longer than I have recently. Stroking her hair. Rocking back and forth. Absolutely adoring her. I know there is confusion and resistance on her part about this voice free experience. That's okay. Resistance is part of the human experience. I wrote to her this morning when she was mad at me for doing this. Explaining I was being too critical of them. Nit picking and nagging. I wrote to her that I am on a mysterious experience, and something is going to be healed. Lessons will be revealed. I don't think she bought it. It will be interesting to see if she can begin to recognize behaviour of others shouldn't take away her peace. Wouldn't that be an awesome tidbit to have at a young age? I send her Love and Light and hope that this experience will be for the Highest Good of All concerned.

I also learned something about forgiveness. I have struggled in my life with being able to forgive. Somehow there was more familiar comfort in holding a grudge and a belly full of poison. We've all heard the adages about how we don't forgive for the person who wronged us, we forgive for ourselves, yadda yadda yadda. Which can sometimes be a pretty tough sell. I worked on forgiveness a lot this week. I didn't go into the experience anticipating to do so. It wasn't even an intention. More a side effect of exploring judgements. One single shift resulting in another shift and another. When you are examining why you feel a particular way, stuff tends to come out of the woodwork. Since I had no interest in holding the wrongdoing in my mind, I had the unexpected opportunity to practice a lot of forgiveness.

You know what really pisses me off? When you really want to forgive but somehow you just can't let it go. It's forgiveness or it's not. You can't forgive then still hold frustration about the situation. It's forgiveness or it's not.

I stumbled onto a game changer for my mental landscape. Since I recognized that there were things I wanted to forgive, yet was struggling to release, I simply forgave myself for the struggle.

I simply **forgave myself for the struggle!!**

Somehow by having compassion and forgiving the resistance, it deflated the animosity and the pressure to forgive. I don't want to say it aloud, let the gremlins in my mind hear... but I think by offering absolution to myself, I shifted into forgiveness! Shhhhh! I'm still processing that one. It is still beneath the Inner Critic's radar.

In the kitchen one of My Little Roommates addresses her sibling, "You know we're good right?" The other replies apprehensively, "No,

I was not aware of that…". She asks, "Are you in agreement?". A considerate contemplative pause, "Yes," the other concedes, "I suppose I am". This is life in an Ocean of Estrogen. I am learning not to interject within their scuffles. They are old enough to work it out themselves. The resumption of chatter between them. I am so very grateful.

<u>January 27:</u>   **DAY SEVEN OF SILENCE**

Today is the birthdate of an estranged now deceased family member. An abuser. A pedophile. Walking wounded himself. Hurting people hurt people.

I find it *interesting* to note that this is my final date of silence. I never took this anniversary into consideration when embarking on this quiet journey. *Isn't that interesting!?* As a child having to be quiet about repeatedly being molested. Here I am quiet yet again. Today I am grateful for the unfolding layers of my healing. I am an adult. I am safe. I am at peace. I remind myself this no longer holds any power over my present. I send him, and all others that were involved, Love and Light, and release it immediately.

In the sifting, sorting and shuffling of my internal beliefs I've come to recognize I continue in somewhat of a splintered state. I do not let anyone see me in my entirety; I fragment myself. Afraid of being shunned, judged or harshly criticized, I restrict my expression. This is a disservice to both myself and those I am interacting with. It's not my job to censor myself to accommodate those on the receiving end. I vow this will be my year of integration.

> I have no more fragmented offerings,
>
> no more splintered shards of Self.
>
> Behold, my kaleidoscope of broken pieces.
>
> Light seeping through my ever shifting voids.

I take a deep breath, and with tears streaming down my face, I return to gratitude.

January 28:

"I sure am grateful you're talking again Mama."

I too am grateful that the experience is behind me and that I have returned to the land of the speaking. I hope I will remember to mindfully bring the insights gained in the quiet quest along: Is it true? Is it kind? Is it necessary.

PS: My child initiated a conversation with a sentence that began "I sure am grateful...."!!!

Thumpity thump thump
Thumpity thump thump
Beats my grateful, grateful heart.

January 29:

I am grateful for a fully stocked pantry.

Looking at my now emptied wallet and a near zero bank account, it is an easy inclination to feel destitute. I challenge myself not to default into poverty mentality. I have converted one form of Energy (currency) into another stockpile of Energy (my fully stocked pantry).

Amongst other things tonight, I am grateful for my cozy blanketed nest of a bed. For my early morning writing. For my game of hide and go seek with my favourite writing pen.

January 30:

I have been bravely practicing setting boundaries. When I feel physically uncomfortable it is the *first* signal something is off. Individuals who have been sexually abused as children have essentially been programmed to disregard our own personal boundaries. When our boundaries of personal space have not been respected, or perhaps when we have bravely dared to speak out and weren't believed, we learn maladjusted ways. It takes a great deal of relearning and reprogramming to first *recognize* when our boundaries are being violated. To realize that it isn't supposed to be that way. To learn to speak up on behalf of our own best interest.

I practiced setting a boundary today. It wasn't comfortable. But I did it. I am so proud of myself when I see how far I have come. I am tremendously grateful.

January 31:

Despite my loathing for the telephone I did something different today! I called a woman I would like to get to know better and possibly develop a friendship with. I am stretching and practicing. I am doing things differently. I am excited by the possibility of me getting out of my own way and I am grateful I stretched beyond my comfort zone.

February
2016

*"DEAR INTUITION,
YOU WANT ME TO WHAT?!"*

February 1:

I have no idea where *any* of this is going. I have decided that's okay. I am trying not to judge myself and am focusing on releasing self-imposed expectations. I don't have to know what tomorrow, or next week, will bring me. I am practicing compassion, acceptance, breathing, and trusting. I am grateful for trying to be flexible.

February 2:

Today is the ancient festival commemorating the cyclical spiral of growth: Imbolc. Mother Earth is slowly awakening from her Winter slumber. Turning towards the arrival of Spring and the return of new growth. I lose myself in the soft glow from an illuminated selenite crystal lamp. Thinking of the frost and snowflakes that will soon melt from strengthening Light. As it is outside, it is also on the inside. I am grateful for all that is melting away, and the promise of new growth.

February 3:

As I stand in the kitchen I am grateful for the sound of rain falling, the smell of fresh brewed morning coffee in the air and a fleeting nanosecond of stillness on a school morning. There is poetry in the pauses.

February 4:

I am grateful for the reminder from the Universe not to be a nitpicky critical parent. My first priority is to be gentle and accepting of who they are. I want to encourage not to criticize or shame. I want them to feel in the very marrow of their bones (without any doubt) that I am in their corner. I want to be their safe place to fall. Not someone constantly focusing on how they aren't doing something right. I am listening. I am learning. Thank you for the reminder. Mother Father

Creator, please help me implement all I am learning. Please help me be the mother I want to be. Please help me raise them for the Highest Good of All involved. I am grateful for the reminders and to dare to learn new ways.

February 5:

Today I did something I have never done before. I treated myself to an Energy healing session with one of the Souls that came through the store on my last day of employment. Being softly touched without any unspoken agenda is a new experience. My toes were held! Have my toes *ever* been held? There were times that I felt myself about to leave my body, but I inhaled deeply, and softly encouraged myself to be as present as I could. To know I was utterly safe. To receive. To breathe and trust. My reprogramming continues. I am grateful.

February 7:

The gentleman I was romantically involved with last year mailed one of My Little Roommates a birthday card. I was moved by his considerate gesture. We connect on the telephone after being out of touch for a couple of months. I am grateful for the opportunity to have connected. It was good to hear his voice again.

February 8:   NEW MOON

★ NEW MOON INTENTIONS

- NEW MOON. NEW CYCLE. NEW ENERGIES. NEW INTENTIONS.
- HOW DO I WANT TO FEEL THROUGHOUT THIS MONTH?
- WHAT AM I PRIORITIZING FOR THIS NEW CYCLE?
- WHAT DO I WANT TO ACCOMPLISH?

In continuing with releasing all that no longer serves, my intention this month is to be open to change. However it presents. Facilitating the exploration of what I believe I am being called to do. It is hard to aspire to be open to a calling... when you can't articulate what the calling is. I know I am feeling called to share my gifts. I have professional training I am not utilizing. I want to. I want to work with women, want to inspire change. I'm no longer interested in working for someone else's dream. I want to explore how I can create my own means of income. I feel as though I am playing a cosmic game of hot and cold with the Universe. Remember that searching game: when you are being prompted by another as to whether or not you are "cold" or "getting warmer" in your pursuit? All I know for certain is I am to pay very close attention to how I feel. My emotions will be the hot or cold. When I identify circumstances in which I feel positive, I am heading the right direction.

February 9:

"Help me find my family" the Facebook post advertised. A young girl looking for her older half siblings. Can anyone help her find her family?

She was looking for me.

In my twenties I experienced a rare but severe side effect to a contraceptive injection: Depo-Provera psychosis. It involved debilitating haunting flashbacks of childhood sexual abuse. Memories I had always had but could no longer keep at bay. This experience, what I dubbed the dark night of my Soul, lasted approximately two years and turned my life upside down. If I was going to survive, I had to face my shadow. Do some ugly work. Ugly icky cringy shadow work.

During intensive psychotherapy I wrote a series of letters to the perpetrator. Angry letters. Angstful letters. Heartbroken letters. Letters I never had any intention of mailing. They were a means of processing and I kept them in the back of my bedroom closet.

One day I did mail them. It would likely be the closest I could ever come to confronting him.

Weeks later I received a note in return, "I received your letters and am working on a reply."

I never heard anything more.

Until two years later, when I received a birth announcement in the mail. He, his new wife, and her five children were excited to announce the arrival of newborn twins. *Her five children.* Knowing the potential danger they were in living with him, my stomach dropped to my feet. I telephoned Child Protective Services in the state the envelope had been postmarked from. Explained to them who I was. Gave them what limited information I had. Would they please investigate to ensure the children in the home were safe.

Rationally I figured I would likely hear from the children, half-siblings, one day. Today was that day.

"Help me find my family."

The door knob to a strained period of life rattles in my hand wanting to burst open. I click "send message". I breathe. I trust. I cha cha cha. Calling on all my Angels and Spirit Guides for support. Please help me handle this with grace.

I focus on my gratefuls.

February 10:

A friend tells me her family is having to move unexpectedly. She comments on the difficulties her family is having in finding a house to rent with this current rental shortage crisis. When she told me this I am flooded with relief that we are not having to move. Yet just as quickly the mysterious red monopoly house that appeared inexplicably in my kitchen cupboard back in December comes to mind.

Tonight I am grateful for a fully stocked pantry. Easy access to clean running water. I am grateful to be surrounded by my loved ones. I am grateful for the freedom to make my own life choices. All that I could ever possibly need to meet my basic physical needs is within an arm's reach.

February 11:

It is one of My Little Roommate's birthday today. There is so much love in her big brown eyes. I am honoured to have her with me in this lifetime. My greatest hope is for My Little Roommates to have a childhood they don't have to recover from.

Tonight I am grateful for: opportunity, self-awareness and conscious choice.

February 12:

Many many moons ago when I began my personal healing journey a wonderfully wise psychotherapist told me it would come in layers. *"Sort of like an artichoke"* she told me. *"You'll think you're done, but lo and behold, there is another layer"* then she laughed a hearty albeit slightly menacing belly laugh before amending her statement, *"No, it's not an artichoke! Healing is a great big onion!! Artichokes won't make you cry".*

I used to roll out my story of survival sharing it with anyone. In the hope of feeling heard, understood, empathized with.... to be believed.

I have a lot of stories in my head that I have been dealing with regarding what I am capable of. Telling myself what I do or don't have to offer the world. Most of the stories originate in a distorted sense of worth.

What I recently discovered, to my surprise, is that if my mind holds the flame of these stories, my body is the base of the burning torch. The handle if you will. While I have been repro-gramming my mental space, my body has continued to hold these stories for me.

Today I realized my life got knocked on its ear last month so that I would have the time, the space and the opportunity for my body to release. For me to do the work that I am called to do, my body, mind and Spirit need to be in alignment and integrated as one.

I have been quite surprised by the sudden and unannounced pres-ence of tears as of late. I am learning to allow the flow of release without judgement and without shame. My body is simply releasing stuck Energy that it has been carrying in a perpetually clenched state for far too long.

It was hip exercises and pelvic floor lifts in yoga class this morning that brought my body to what it needed to release. No shame, no awkwardness. Just subtle silent tears flowing behind long loose hair in my face. No explanation, no offering, no comment to my class-mates. Just subtle silent flow of tears. I will no longer clench to keep them at bay. My body wants to release and so it is time. It is time for this beautiful sacred container of mine to release.

Tonight I am grateful my body was patient enough to wait for me to reconnect. To hold the space patiently without breaking down and demanding my attention. Thank you body, for all the gazillions of functions you perform on my behalf without any instruction or appreciation on my behalf. Thank you, I love you. I come in peace. Finally.... I come in peace.

Thank you. I love you.

February 13:

Full circle moment. My Little Roommates have friends sleeping over and they are dancing to Eminem's 'Lose Yourself'. Reflecting on where I was in life when that came out. Remembering the manic angst I carried in my heart and mind. When the song first appeared on the air waves I was a mere five years into my personal healing journey. I was trying not to self-harm or sabotage as my stormy marriage was finally dwindling to an end. I wrap my arms around myself and give thanks for my journey of healing. I give thanks for my personal growth.

Tonight I am grateful for the power of a song. The backdrop soundtracks to our lives and the snapshot freeze frame memories they can hold. Progress checks along the winding road of life.

February 14:

I took the time to meditate in a corner of the house this evening. I was astonished at how it seemed to mellow everyone's Energy just a bit, even the dog. I laugh because for years I so adamantly resisted meditation. I only began to explore it during my silent experience.

Tonight I am grateful for the realization that when I resist something with an inexplicable level of intensity, it needs to be explored. Explored without judgement and with a heaping dose of detached curiosity. Extreme resistance is a flashing neon sign there is something I need to explore. I am learning.

February 15:

I am grateful for poems born on the forest trail...

"This way"
She calls me
"To the person you want to be"
"The vision you are unfolding into"
"This way".

Extending her hand
Encouraging my reach
"This way"
"one more step"
"one more mindful choice."

She prods me out of inaction.
"Are you facing the right direction?"
"Are you headed the right way?"
"Can you feel it in your bones?"
She lifts me from a tired heap on the floor,
Straightens me up,
Lovingly dusts me off.
"Up you, come along now..."
"This way"
"This way"
And through the woods we go
trusting my growth will be supported.

February 16:

Tonight I am grateful for "eureka!" moments. Recognizing nuggets of ancient truth camouflaged as trite cliché. Let's face it. They become clichés for a reason.

February 17:

I prepared a nourishing meal today: roast turkey, brown rice, fresh vegetables. There are so many things that so many don't experience on a daily basis. I am so very grateful for the privilege of easily feeding my family.

My Little Roommates and I took a quiet moment to hold thankful hearts for all of our blessings. To hold gratitude for all the amazing things on their way to us, that we don't have a clue about. It was neat to involve my children in that moment, holding the Energy and hope together. Expecting miracles.

February 18:

I stood there this morning on the forest trail, stopped in my tracks. Face to face with the latest metaphor in my life as of late. The footbridge leading to my favourite part of the forest had been washed away. The section was enchanted. You could *feel* the faeries and elementals dancing just out of sight. The ground a thick carpet of lichens and moss, the tree canopy overhead nearly cathedral. The way it held the dew and rain was captivating. With recent heavy rains and winds the entire embankment simply slipped into the rushing creek taking the bridge down with it. In a fleeting moment of defeat, I turned with dog, our heads hung low with disappointment, and trudged our way back up to the main trail.

I am at a crossroads. The unknown swirls about me. But in this pungent moment of unknown, magick and possibility await. *One cannot exist without the other.* The only question remains. What am I going to consciously focus on: the ground coming out from under my feet, or the flow of potential and rebirth? Both exist for me right now. Which will it be? *"Be brave"* I whispered to myself, *"I am being redirected."* I remind myself, I asked for this. I dared to invoke Kali-Ma to destroy all that did not serve, so that I could dare to rebuild.

Whatever perspective I hold, I will absolutely find evidence to support it. That's where my power lies. If I look for the beautiful bright side, I will find it! If I look for evidence that the Universe is compassionate and has my back, I will find evidence to support it! Just as with the other extreme. Except the other extreme *is so in our face* that one doesn't have to be swayed.

It doesn't have to be that way. So with that, I very intentionally choose to keep refocusing. I twist and I turn. Mindfully refocusing my soulful kaleidoscope over and over and over again to focus on the magick, the beauty, and practice radical gratitude.

Right about now you may be wondering up what is with magick with a 'K'. Allow me a moment to explain. There is magic and there is magick. Magic involves parlour tricks, sleight of hand. Perhaps rabbits out of top hats. Magick is the art of influencing change through Energy, our inherent personal power and harnessing Universal Laws. I get very passionate about our abilities to empower change and love teaching the concept of personal co-creation.

Back to my gratitude. Tonight I am grateful that I ever had the experience of knowing that mysterious part of the forest. I am grateful for washed away bridges. For crossroads and redirection. I am grateful for pungent moments of deep unknowing and the fertile potential that begins to gurgle from murky depths like a lotus.

February 19:

Oh my beautifully strong willed teenage Little Roommates! They are the fiery blue core of the Bunsen burner flame beneath my beaker of Life. They bring me to a bubbling frothy boil and are two of the most powerful catalysts of my personal alchemy.

Resistance is futile. Expansion non-negotiable. These wise, sensitive, exquisitely tender old Souls, whose unfolding cannot be described with words. They turn me inside out and upside down and I am all the better for it! They are the storm, the starry sky, the ocean, the void and everything in between. The pair are my greatest teachers and greatest challenges. I am grateful.

February 20:

Change is stirring. I have absolutely no idea what is coming down the pike but I can feel it in my bones. I twist and turn, twist and turn, *twist and turn* my soulful kaleidoscope until I find the perspective of gratitude. Tonight, I am grateful simply for my willingness to find gratitude.

February 21:

Last December one of My Little Roommates telephoned me at work in a panic to tell me that a tree had fallen, grazing the house on the way down.

"Did the roof come in?"

"No"

"Are the walls intact?"

"Yes"

"Then I will see it when I come home"

When I pulled up that night I expected to see a large limb had fallen or perhaps a significant branch. But when I reached the top of the driveway, I was shocked to find a full sized evergreen tree, more than forty feet tall with a circumference of nearly three feet around perched precariously down the sloped lot. Had I been home when it fell, my car would have been parked where it landed and the vehicle would have been crushed. I was amazed this tree hadn't come through the roof.

Friends and community members didn't really believe me about the size of the tree in my yard until they saw it for themselves. This enormous tree lay feet from the front porch. We adapted by going out the side door. It became a new highway path for local squirrels. I did my best to keep my kids off of it. I tried to practice patience and hold hope regarding its anticipated removal but I eventually resorted to referring to it as installation art.

As of late I have been wondering if in my decade of being an independent parent I missed the opportunity to model co-existence to My Little Roommates. I don't want them growing up with a *my way or the highway* mentality because they never saw their mother having to negotiate or compromise. Things have been tight financially since my sudden unemployment and I am unable to continue living comfortably with the level of expenses that I have.

Having recently reconnected with an ex-boyfriend after he mailed My Little Roommate a birthday card, I know he has been unable to find an appropriate house mate. It didn't come to me immediately, but in the days after speaking with him, Intuition started to whisper. I am inclined to rent space from him in an effort to reduce monthly expenses for everyone. I figure we are friends, I certainly trust him more than most. We are mature adults. Why not work together to create ease? I am unnerved by this Intuitive prompting but, strangely, I don't have an ounce of hesitation. After a family meeting with My Little Roommates, we have decided that we will vacate at the end of the month when our lease expires and will rent a section of his large cabin in the hopes of creating a win-win opportunity.

Anyone I share this plan with thinks I am nuts! Peppering me with questions that I am not able to logically answer, "*the monopoly house in the cupboard, the fallen tree, and the whisper in the back of my mind tell me to do this*". Maybe I am nuts! But at least I am nuts with good intentions. At least I am respecting a promise I made to my 'Beloved I Am Presence', my Source Energy, and my Intuition: *thy will be done.*

Like many times so far this year I have the sensation I am a meteor bursting brilliantly through the night sky. I quiver with uncertainty, but I feel strongly guided by Intuition.

I am being redirected. I breathe, and I trust and I cha cha cha.

February 22:   FULL SNOW MOON

★ FULL MOON REFLECTIONS:

- HAVE MY FEELINGS THE PAST TWO WEEKS BEEN CONSISTENT WITH WHAT I IDENTIFIED AS MY DESIRED FEELINGS AT THE NEW MOON?
- HAVE I TAKEN ACTIONS CONSISTENT WITH THE DIRECTION I WISH TO GO?

Well.... I said my intention was to remain open to embracing change. At this point, I am certainly heeding my Intuition or else I am listening to my own delusional ramblings. I am nervous. Not much of this makes sense. But I can't help but feel this is the right direction. For what, I've no idea. I can't help but chuckle reminiscing at the strange foreshadowing of the monopoly house in the cupboard.

I am proud that My Little Roommates and I are making brave compassionate choices and stretching beyond their own routine comfort zones. One of My Little Roommates was clever enough to put an addendum clause as part of our decision to move, *"If we move away from my friends, can I have them over for a weekend campout sometime during the summer?"*

Adventure is most certainly in the air.

February 23:

I am grateful to have connected with the friend we will be renting from, herein referred to as the co-tenant, and established a moving day plan. My lease is up in a matter of days, I am navigating a huge undertaking on a tight timeline.

February 24:

I did something new again today! A woman who I have not met, but have mutual friends with, needed transportation to the mainland where she is having surgery. By driving her into town, I have a free ferry crossing, thereby creating the opportunity to stock up on more affordable groceries in the city. It was a long day, but she was a delightful character, and we had a wonderful time! It was so strange driving past places and going down memory lane: the hospital My Little Roommates were both born in, the first house my oldest remembers, and the one I brought the youngest home to from the hospital. I begin to cry, but try to be discreet. I'm not sad, it's just weird seeing it all again. Another progress report on how far I have come. Grateful for the opportunity to help someone out, and in turn, be helped by her.

February 25:

I am grateful the space we are moving into is being emptied of the co-tenant's belongings and his storage solutions of stacked cardboard boxes. I am relieved by the unprompted gesture. I will not nag. I remind myself martyrdom comes in many different forms.

I am grateful for the opportunity to do this differently.

February 26:

I have so much on my list of things to do! So many errands, responsibilities and moving preparations demanding my attention. But what needs my attention the most in this stressful moment: is taking the opportunity to care for myself. I am grateful I squeezed in a pocket of self-care: a long hike in my favourite patch of forest with dog. I am learning to opt for self-care over martyrdom. For that I am *truly* and profoundly grateful.

February 27:

I am grateful for new opportunities and swift change. I am terrified. I am exhilarated. I am grateful.

February 28:

I am grateful for late night one on one hangout time with one of My Little Roommates, I feel so blessed.

March
2016

"On the move"

Note to Reader: There was a gap in my grateful entries between March 1ˢᵗ and March 7ᵗʰ as we moved homes and towns.

March 8:   NEW MOON
                                      TOTAL SOLAR ECLIPSE

Moving day and I am sore and utterly exhausted. While most of our belongings are in our space, some of them remain outside on the driveway covered and tethered beneath a tarp.

As weary as I am I make a conscious point to be mindful of the time. At 5:58pm, the exact moment of the eclipse, I stand on a pine needle covered driveway. A wind rising, a light rain shower beginning. I clear my mind, anchor myself within my heart and release my wildest hopes and dreams into the great beyond: *to create a life and career that is built upon the foundation of my creativity, my spirituality, my expression, and my coaching training.*

I imagine rainbow hued bubbles of prayer, Love and Light swirling around my body. Beginning at my feet, twirling about me as they rise, up, up, up! Around my legs, hips and upper body before up, up, up! Catching the wind, floating into the great beyond to grow and thrive.

With this New Moon and change of residence, I declare it my intention to lessen the burden. Thereby increasing greater possibility of freedom for expansion, for all parties involved. To help myself and at the same time assist a friend. To broaden our perspectives. To create win-win.

Thank you North. Thank you East. Thank you South. Thank you West. Thank you Above, and thank you Below. Thank you Within, and thank you Without. Thank you Mother Father Creator. Thank you my 'Beloved I Am Presence'. Thank you for the whisperings of Spirit that have prompted this new adventure. I am so deeply grateful for all that is being set into motion, that as of this moment, I have no idea about.

I hold a crazy heart oversaturated and dripping with gratitude.

March 9:

The morning after a move always has that moment of confusion. When you awake with sleep still encrusted in your eyes. That moment when you aren't sure where you are before clarity joins you.

Today I am grateful for the opportunity to help a friend; for the hope to create flowing ease for ALL involved. I am grateful that we got as many of our belongings in yesterday as we did before the rains came. I am grateful I was able to return the truck in a timely fashion. But more importantly: I am grateful I don't have to lift a couch again today.

March 10:

In my many years of independent parenting this is now my sixth move. Not bragging by any means, but I will not wear shame either. It is what it is.

Observations from a nomadic existence: Feeling settled is important to me. Non-negotiable. I will unpack like a woman obsessed until it comes to be. I have had landlords come in mere days after a move and be shocked with my progress. *"It looks like you've been here for years"*.

My system is this. Establish the general location for big pieces of furniture. Don't get attached to the placement. All is unfolding. Unpack the boxes. Doesn't have to be organized. Doesn't have to have a home. But sweet in tarnation: the boxes need to be gone.

We shuffle, and we sort. We shuffle, and we sort. We move boxes from room to room.

"Have you seen the _____?"
"Not yet."

"Have you seen the _____?"
"Not yet."

"Have you seen the _____?"
"Not yet."

But then.... Then that marvelous moment of excited victory finally happens:

"Have you seen the _____?"
"Yes- yes I have!!!"
The crowd goes wild!

Oh wait. You want me to be able to tell you where it actually is?? Perhaps I will know its location tomorrow.

Tonight I am grateful for progress in our shuffling and sorting. The rediscovery of our belongings has begun! I am grateful for that awesome moment: Yes, yes I have seen that!

March 11:

In the continued process and progress of shuffling and sorting, one of My Little Roommates smiled *so deeply* this evening, I saw dimples I didn't know existed!

I wonder how she kept that secret for as long as she did. She is an enigmatic creature of mystery, that one. Nice to meet you dimples! You are exquisite hanging there like the moon beneath a field of stars and sparkling eyes.

March 13:

More and more of my family's moving boxes are being unpacked. With every cardboard box emptied, flattened, and removed from our space, I become more and more excited at the possibility of making it feel like home. I am a nester. I need to create a cozy welcoming ambience. It is important that my home be a reflection of myself and that it rise up to greet me joyously when I walk through the door.

March 14:

Today is the first day of Spring Break and it coincides with the beginning of daylight savings time and changing the clocks ahead by an hour. Thank goodness for easy time transitions. Tonight I am grateful for ease and flow.

March 15:

Since the move I've been trying to find our portable DVD player. With no bedroom walls or door to define my own space, all I want to do is pop in a movie, slide on a pair of headphones, and create some form of solitude whilst curling up in my bed.

Today it happened: I finally found that sought after DVD player! I am grateful to be bumping self-care to my top priority.

March 16:

There are no bathroom facilities in our attic. No big deal, walk downstairs and use the bathroom there. But having to engage in small talk with each passage of the stairwell every time nature calls is quickly becoming irksome.... *eight days in*.

I am also having to share an established kitchen with a long term bachelor. I haven't shared a kitchen in nearly a decade. There are things *growing things* in a refrigerator that could best be described as a science experiment gone horribly awry. Joint custody of cupboards are uncovering the discovery of packages with expiry dates from years ago. I knew, going in, that there would be negotiations, compromise, and stretching boundaries. I guess that is the phase where it is now at.... *eight days in*.

I laugh at the possibility that My Little Roommates may adjust more easily to a shared household than I will.

Regardless I spent the afternoon in the passenger seat of the co-tenant's car: mutual errands, cooperation, progress, momentum. This is doable. I got this. But I can't shake the feeling, that I have jumbled up the order of life events. You meet. You date. You fall in love. Then you move in.

You don't move in *after* a breakup to try and help one another out. You *don't* add the pressure of becoming a roommate. Want to know why? Oh, at this point, even at *just eight days in*, I can offer about ten thousand examples. Namely: everything that ever bugged you during the relationship, that's why! This will either go down in my personal history as being the stupidest thing I have ever done. Or the most compassionate thing I have ever done. My own assessment varies by the minute.

Meet. Friends. Date. Fall in love. *Then* move in.

I should write this down in permanent marker somewhere. Maybe tattoo it on my body for future reference. Too late now. We will label this as *"seemed like a good idea at the time"*. I will focus on things to be grateful for. I'm an adult. I can do this.

Why do I hear laughter in the darkest depths of my brain?

And why are there motorcycle parts and a dissected lamp on the kitchen counter?

Adventure is in the air. Find the gratefuls. Find the gratefuls.

March 17:

The co-tenant came up into the attic and mounted wall shelves for me. Tonight I am grateful for cooperation and the opportunity to create a sense of home. The nesting and unfolding continues!

I am also grateful that I have been purging the refrigerator of expired opened jars. Culling the moldy herd. Though there has been protest. But I refuse to scrape a centimetre of green fuzz off of the contents to consume the rest. So I do what any peace loving mature adult would do: I wait until no one is looking. Stuff a jar of expired tartar sauce in my purse to be disposed of at another time at another location.

I feel like a drug lord smuggling contraband. But I will prevail. Shared fridge. Room has to be made. Apparently, it's up to me. I will not gripe about what is not within my control, instead, I will harness what influence I have.

I am grateful for stealth like progress, ingenuity, a deep purse and sidewalk garbage cans.

March 18:

A friend asked if I could watch her daughter today. It has been rather strange to say the least, adapting to sharing a home with someone else. I am uncertain how to add another child to the mix so I opted to take the kids to the public swimming pool. I was delighted to discover it was a $2 public swim. Awesome!

Savoured the hot tub. Frolicked with my girls. Did something different and slid down the indoor water slide splashing and giggling all the way.

Tonight I am grateful for the happy miracles that present as simple everyday moments. I love how this Grateful Jar Project has me diligently seeking out moments of wonder seemingly camouflaged as everyday simplicity.

March 19:

Swimming

There is a poem here, a memory
Playing out before me
I savour it; intoxicating.
Submerged in the swimming pool
Brown eyes sparkling and mischievous
Blue eyes seeking out the other
Aquatic hide and seek.
Arms wrap around my neck
The other clamours atop shoulders
Entangled limbs flailing and splashing
Shrieks of delight and mock terror
Chlorine strong in the air.
There is a poem here, a memory
If, once home, I can recapture it
Amongst domestic chaos; bliss.

March 20:

The last cardboard box left my space today!! I have moved an entire house worth into a long large open attic. I am now exploring creating zones, using larger pieces to help establish parameters of where one space ends and another begins.

Tomorrow will be the first day of Spring. To commemorate the change of season, and celebrate the accomplishment of being completely unpacked, I sage our space. Then I sit channelling love to my houseplants after their arduous journey. Houseplants never like moving. Hell, who does??

March 21:   FIRST DAY OF SPRING

Tiny green shoots are appearing on the tree outside our attic window. Goodbye Winter, thank you for all you shared with us. I marvel at all the sudden dramatic changes navigated through one season alone. Hello Spring!! Thank you for tangible signs of new growth and change.

March 22:

One season into the Grateful Jar Project. While there are days I've missed, I am proud of my discipline thus far. To ensure the continuity of the habit, I mount a note *"Have you done your gratefuls?"* on the slanted ceiling atop the bedside table that houses my Grateful Jar. The jar sits there in its new home surrounded by art and crystals. A little altar unto itself. An altar of gratitude. What I think, I create. I will use these powers for good.

I am disheartened that no action has been taken to create a shared environment within the communal kitchen. Perhaps it's only my priority. A lot of the belongings that were moved out of the space we now inhabit, landed in the kitchen. I had assumed that was a temporary solution. Anything I have ever learned about making assumptions, namely that expression "make an ass out of you and me" is being reinforced. I wonder if there ever comes a time in our development when no assumptions are made at all? I reassure myself I am learning much about expectations and communicating honestly and clearly.

Uncertain how to proceed or navigate such a strange circumstance, I embark on a game of cardboard box Jenga to clear a wider berth in the main travel path. I wonder if the unused exercise bike will always live wedged against the kitchen table? And how long will we have to navigate towers of cardboard boxes containing miscellaneous items before sitting down to eat?

It is days like these when I am flooded by uncertainty that it is imperative I find gratitude.

March 23:   **FULL WOLF MOON**

★ FULL MOON REFLECTIONS

- HAVE MY EMOTIONAL EXPERIENCES THIS CYCLE BEEN WHAT I SET FORTH AS MY NEW MOON INTENTION?
- HOW WILL I INFLUENCE MY EMOTIONAL EXPERIENCE?
- IS THERE SOMETHING I CAN RELEASE?
- WHAT WILL I DELEGATE?
- HOW WILL I ASK FOR ASSISTANCE OR SUPPORT?

Admittedly I am finding this strange strained adjustment far more stressful than I anticipated. How can I begin to sway this? The Grateful Jar Project started with me identifying three things from the last 24 hours I'm grateful for. I am challenging myself to now identify five each day. Life gets hard. Play harder. When I look over my grateful list at the end of the night they aren't monumental things I am recording. More often than not I am finding gratitude for details, blessings and good fortunes that are so easily overlooked. Things we are so accustomed to they are easily taken for granted.

We spent the day in our attic space, pantless and/or in varying stages of undress. In an unusual treat, the co-tenant has left the house for the day and I got to savour one on one time with My Little Roommates. No obligatory small talk on the way to the bathroom! Free to absolutely be ourselves... free to roam pantless!!! I never thought I could be so grateful for an afternoon of us not wearing pants.

Long may it be the power of three: Grateful, grateful, grateful.

March 24:

A new job today! Opportunities and possibilities! Early shift. Early, early, EARLY shift... 6am start. Yikes!!

Grateful? Yes, I remind myself: grateful. This early shift wouldn't even be a possibility without another adult available to assist if necessary.

March 25:

There is huge contrast in the different lifestyles co-existing inside this cabin. Tonight I am deeply grateful for our own space. Zones. Candles. Comfort. Mini nests. I am not interested in harping or nagging the co-tenant to clean up. I will harness whatever influence I have over my own surroundings.

I call upon my Angels, my Spirit Guides, my Mother Father Creator. Please, please help me to see the truth, the sincerity, and the purity within this strange experience of contrast. I am headed for a big lesson. Please allow me to receive it with ease.

Whatever I look for I will find evidence to support.

Am I going to focus on all the different ways I feel disappointment?

Am I going to focus on growing resentment?

Am I going to focus on the behaviours of another?

Or am I going to reclaim my power? Harness control over my perspective. Practice compassion for all.

Am I going to white knuckle it to find my five gratefuls if I have to?

Yes! Yes I am!! Because at the end of the day. That's how I want to feel. Grateful. Bright with hope. Optimistic. Not angry or bitter. I release. I release. I release!! I am grateful I recognize the choice.

March 26:

A friend left on her own moving adventure today, having left from the Fraser Valley and moving to a tiny island on the Gulf Coast. I hold her in the Light wishing her the best on her adventures. I am grateful she has embraced the adventure of change and released herself from a stressful situation. Change is *indeed* in the air for so many these days. May we be brave. May we all heal what needs to be healed, so we may step into that which we are being called to do.

March 27:

The family has settled to the best of our abilities into this strange shared space. Only time can do the rest. My Little Roommates are at their new schools, relatively content and adjusting well.

It is hard trying to feel at home, moving into a pre-established space that overflows with decades and decades of unedited belongings. I dare say I underestimated the impact that would have on my psychological wellness. When the collection of belongings was spread over three different floors, I didn't get a sense of what I was moving us into. But with it all jammed and crammed onto one floor and the middle level of the expansive cabin... I can't even finish this sentence.

It is overwhelmingly devastating to witness and not be able to do anything about it. Better yet, it's not up to me to do anything about it. It's not up to me to tell another how they should live. All I can do is model and encourage. But I have to release all expectations. ALL expectations.

Can I do that?

I think the best way to cope at this point is to create a garden. I need dirt to cope and to maintain balance. If I cannot influence the interior of the home, I can create a sanctuary for myself and My Little Roommates in the yard. Plus, I'll get vegetables out of the deal.

March 28:

The duality and polar extremes of life have never been more starkly evident to me. I feel as though I am being swallowed alive by the jam packed cabin. In response to the overwhelming stagnant clogged Energy, I get us out of the house as often as possible. Twisting and turning, twisting and turning, twisting and turning my soulful kaleidoscope to find the gratitude. It's always there. Sometimes I just have to look a little harder.

My Little Roommates and I sat along the waterfront this afternoon. Watching moored boats gently rocking upon waves, savouring the mixed aromas of creosote and ocean brine. As conversation unfolds I marvel at the unique and vastly different personalities of each of them.

March 29:

I left for work this morning in darkness but was greeted by a slice of crescent moon hanging in the black early morning sky. I am reminded there is subtle beauty everywhere. I just have to be persistent in seeking it.

March 30:

There has been sudden inexplicable concern on the part of the co-tenant regarding the wooden staircase leading to our space. Plans to reinforce the stairwell are underway. I'd rather the Energy be put into clearing the dining area. I don't want to present a lovingly prepared meal amidst stacked towers of musty cardboard boxes. I suppose different people hold different priorities.

It is not up to me to insist someone follows my agenda of expectations. For years I have been able to manage a household and command direction. I do not have that freedom of leadership in this situation. It's not up to me to tell someone what needs to be done. Scratch that. Everyone in this situation *knows* what needs to be done. I am not prepared to nag the task to fruition. I am not interested in assuming that role. I am not interested in engaging in power struggle. I am not interested in fighting about it. While it feels as though it is eating me alive. I do my very best to observe with detachment. To not hook into what I cannot influence.

Tonight I am especially grateful for coping skills. I am grateful for windows. My blood boils anytime I pass through the house and so I am looking out windows a lot. I have to be selective of what windows I look out so my gaze is not cast upon more piles outside.

In this moment I choose to hold the vision that if the stairwell project is such a priority it will be brought to completion. I will choose to embrace the perspective that he is concerned about my family's physical well being, even if it is against impending stairwell attack.

I am grateful for humour.

March 31:

Homemade dinner, previously frozen in one of my particularly planful moments. I am grateful for the ease in pulling it out to defrost today. I am grateful for tiny miracles and moments of strategy and forethought.

April
2016

"TANGLED MOUNDS
AND
INVASIVE GROWTH"

April 1:

Upon cleverly recognizing an April Fool's joke on social media, one of My Little Roommates declares, "I am getting wise in my old age! Sniffing out the antics of young hooligans!" Admittedly, I fell for it hook, line and sinker. I am raising wise ones.

"*Young hooligans*" out of the mouth of babes. I am grateful for the laughter.

April 2:

I've been surveying the progression of sunlight as it stretches across the property that is nestled amongst birch, maple and evergreen trees. The sweet spot of exposure lays in the north east corner; it is an expansive tangled mound more than six feet tall of wild black-berries and other invasive growth.

I need a patch to clear and tend to. To bring forth new life, honouring all the different stages in the spiralled cycle of growth. And so overlooking the daunting nature of my project I approach it with a modest pair of hand clippers.

The co-tenant appears around the side of the cabin inquiring, "Would you like to borrow my electric trimmer?"

It seems I disappoint, or at the very least confuse, when I explain I want to go slowly... mindfully. Expressing that I am introducing myself to this plot of yard. Wooing her. My labour is my sacrificial offering to her. If I resort to the use of a power tool, I won't be able to hear fervent whispered offerings when she makes herself known.

If I were to focus on all of the gargantuan amount of work ahead, I'd be overwhelmed. Instead, I take it one clip at a time. Focusing on little steps, holding the vision I have in my heart for this space. It is like that with all of Life's projects. If we focus on the enormity, it's too easy to stall into inaction. Break it down. Manageable action steps. Still overwhelming? Then there is still a layer to be dissected and reduced even further.

Progress is slow in the making. But after a day of toiling and clearing in the sun I'm grateful for dirt beneath my fingernails, soil smudged across my face, and the earthy womanly smells of my sweaty body. I am grateful for arduous physical undertaking. It exhausts my body and clears my mind. Giving me something to focus on other than the cluttered chaos, stagnant energy, unmet expectations, and burgeoning resentments.

April 3:

Waking at 5am to be at work for 6am is a brutal adjustment, especially when you have no bedroom walls or door in a house full of night owls. I am grateful for earplugs and a sleep mask.

This morning I captured a quiet moment for myself. A fleeting moment claimed seaside at the break of dawn. Matching my breath to rolling ocean waves, deeply inhaling the wonderful aroma of brine. To slip out of my shoes and feel the pebbled beach beneath my feet. Watching seabirds soar as the sky unfolds transforming from lackluster grey dusk into pink dawn.

No matter the time. No matter the circumstance. No matter the location. There is the potential to seize the opportunity for self-care. It is not a treat or a reward. It is a basic necessity. It is powerful medicine. Therapy. I must take the time, if I do not wish to end up *serving* time.

April 4:

Tonight in the shared kitchen I clashed with the co-tenant. We are two adults *very* accustomed to living independently; doing things our own way. I empathize that it cannot be easy having someone move into your home and want to do things differently. Someone that questions the logic. Someone that will not rest on her laurels. Someone that makes stuff happen. If you are resistant to change, that has to be intense. I offer silent compassion.

Tonight I am grateful I got to model compromise to my daughters today with peaceful mature negotiations. Yes, that is how I will spin it: modelling compromise to My Little Roommates.

Holy mashugana. I sure hope they were taking notes.

April 5:

I am finding it increasingly difficult to find gratitude throughout the day. Instead I want to focus on what infuriates me! I find it interesting to observe what a remarkable distraction this is.

The goal was to reduce household overhead. To create new opportunities. To heed Spirit and create my best Life. Here I am busying myself creating a list of all the things that are driving me insane. May I add: it is a *magnificently* extensive list.

But is this how I wish to invest the Energy of my attention?

If I focus on what is driving me mad, I will only see more evidence to support what is driving me mad. If I can shift that perspective, I reclaim my power. Power, that somehow, I unknowingly began leaking everywhere. Here I stand in a goopy puddle of my own unravelling. It's not pretty and it's not empowering.

As my angst stirs I unleash it upon the blackberry thicket out back. Ripping and ravaging thorned vines. Pulling them out by the root until I feel better. Or until I've exhausted myself. I realize that becoming so overly irritated by the behaviours of another, could very well be the ultimate distraction. I am reminding myself that big lessons come from moments of contrast, and in keeping with that: I am in for one *huge* lesson.

Making dozens of clips before I manage to free a single length of prickled vine. Loading the clippings onto a tarp I pull them up a sloped incline to the fire pit. Dragging the cumbersome tarp behind me, like a thorned train trailing in the wake of a sweaty grunting bride on her stoic progression to the altar. I can't help but consider what in Life I am dragging behind me? People. Circumstances. Expectations. Perceived obligations. It's straining. It's draining. I am exhausted pulling all that behind me. How hard do I have to make this for myself? The time has come to release, throw all that is not serving onto the funeral pyre.

Reminding myself I am grateful for the opportunity to heal and resolve the next layer of relationship issues. Self-awareness keeps me curious. This... *this is going to be interesting.*

April 6:

A different training opportunity was presented at work. The late shift. Having only recently adjusted to rising at 5am for the early shift, my bedtime is no longer compatible with not being home until midnight. It has to be either or.

I have silently committed to myself to turn down as many of those shifts as possible. I am learning boundaries. No, this is not what I signed up for. No, this will not work for me.

It is important to me that I be available to My Little Roommates at dinner. We have always eaten together. I won't sacrifice that. More importantly it is my priority to be there at bedtime. To be able to tuck at least one of them in. To hold them in an embrace, loving them in that quiet moment of winding down before sleep.

I am grateful for moments of contrast and profound learning. I am grateful to be identifying what *will* work for me and what *will not.* I am grateful I am recognizing the deal breakers.

April 7:

★ NEW MOON. NEW CYCLE. NEW INTENTIONS:

- HOW DO I WANT TO FEEL THIS COMING LUNAR CYCLE?
- WHAT DO I WANT TO CREATE?
- WHAT ARE MY PRIORITIES TO BE ACCOMPLISHED?
- IS HOW I AM SPENDING MY TIME AND INVESTING MY PERSONAL ENERGY ALIGNED WITH THE ABOVE?

I want to feel progress. Hmmmm. "Progress" isn't an emotion. How do I want to *feel?* I want to feel content. Beautiful... comfortable... relaxed... peaceful. *I want to thrive.* I want to create a positive atmosphere both within and around myself. I want to create a sensory oasis. I want to create the sanctuary of a garden.

Is how I am spending my time and how I am investing my personal Energy aligned with how I want to feel?

My efforts in clearing the garden. Yes. Maintaining my individual family's space within the home. Yes. Sensory oasis? I am beginning to realize this will not be possible in this house. Which has me questioning, *how important is this to me?* What actions am I prepared to take?

I head out to my claimed patch of yard, to dig, to curse, to stomp it out. I offer tears as almsgiving to the thinning thicket as I continue. There must be a decade worth of untamed blackberry growth in this tangled bramble. My arms are scratched and bleeding from my efforts. I am uncertain which is more difficult to remove: the snare of the fresh green growth barbed with large triangle thorns, or the dusty dried undergrowth. The sting to my skin is the same. But the brittle decayed vine snaps away easily. Whereas the newer growth stubbornly resists, snaring itself with its thorned teeth, refusing to be pulled away without struggle.

It strikes me this is an analogy for the human psyche: old beliefs acting as a scaffolding for new stories to climb, to stretch, to thrive. New beliefs pop up through the dirt floor, wrapping themselves around the undergrowth to thrive, choking. Unexamined. Untamed.

April 8:

I am grateful for "adulting". Communication, negotiating, and compromise. Thirty days into this new living situation, I find it interesting to observe how easy it is to have expectations I thought would be common sense. How in my own inability to express them, I have set myself up for disappointment.

Do I release expectations and embrace a *live and let live* philosophy or are these deal-breakers? I worry they may be deal-breakers. When others' behaviours impact us, is that when expectations morph into boundaries? My mind swirls for answers. All I want is the Highest Good of All involved, and while that's not up to me to define what that looks like, I *do* have the right to say "Yeah.... this ain't it".

It is an interesting dichotomy of crazy making. I have begun recognizing what this is costing me mentally. Yet I still insist I can make this work.

Really...Really?!?

Am I making this harder?

April 9:

Appreciating that everything I say and do has a ripple effect in my mind and my life, I practice being mindful. Very carefully being aware of all of my dialogues.

I am grateful for self-awareness.

April 10:

Getting ready in the dark early hours of morning I am grateful for the smell of freshly ground coffee beans. The gurgling symphony as the machine steams, freshly ground beans percolating, then followed by the aroma of fresh brewed coffee. The sensory nuances of a morning ritual and a day slowly unfolding into action. We are surrounded by beauty if we wish to look for it. Celebrate it.

My new place of employment is a positive easy going atmosphere. What a delightful experience: not having to walk on eggshells, not trying to anticipate what mood swing you will have to dodge today.

April 11:

Ahead of schedule on this dark and dreary morning, I sat in my car at the ocean's edge. My windows rolled down watching daybreak slowly spread across dark sky. Savouring seagulls riding the wind, the sound of waves crashing, as I focus on the rise and fall of my breath. Powerful medicine to nourish a weary Soul.

April 12:

There is much to be learned from this experience of cohabitation. Most specifically I am recognizing the profound impact physical environments have.

My preference would be to avoid his level of the cabin altogether. When I am there, I find myself wanting to lash out at him angrily. Blood frothing and boiling wanting to crawl out of my skin in response to the disarray.

Unfortunately the joint kitchen is ground zero of this stockpiled shamble. When I go in to cook, I set up a small temporary altar on a cleared section of windowsill. A stick of incense burning, a framed drawing of Ganesh; most appropriately, the Hindu deity of overcoming obstacles. Accompanied by a statue of the Divine

Feminine, usually either Our Lady of Guadalupe, Sarasvati, or Tara. A lit candle and a handful of small tumbled crystals. Shifting my focus away from the static of virulence, decay and neglect I am standing in. Instead intently concentrating on shielding my stovetop creations. Mindfully infusing my cooking with Love and Light as I stir, ground and shield.

I feel myself slipping into a martyred victim mindset. Is it too much to want my family to sit at a dinner table without having to clamour and climb over cardboard boxes or scale an exercise bike to sit on their chair?? Clearly I had unspoken expectations. There's a lesson in this for me: *clearly communicate my expectations.* I catch myself berating myself for how I could have ever just written this off as eclectic collecting.

Having recognized an unempowered mindset creeping in, I refuse to engage in self-deprecating thoughts. What I think is what I create. I will not judge myself. I will not criticize myself. I will hold as tight as I can to compassion and forgiveness. My Grateful Jar will be my floatation device. Beating myself up internally will only compound my frustrations.

Very consciously I choose to harness whatever influence I have over the situation. Since I quite clearly cannot change the condition of the house I commit to being mindful of my self-talk. Doing everything I can to keep myself and My Little Roommates buoyant during our time here.

April 13:

Maybe it's a co-dependent thing. Maybe it's a caregiver thing. Maybe it's a martyr thing. I am observing how much I want to assist those around me by "doing for them."

Life is like a dinner plate: It can only hold so much. When I start saying *"here, let me do this for you"* there's that much less room on my plate for what I want. When my plate is overloaded, it's inevitable something is going to slide off and land on the floor. I am choosing to be mindful of the distractions I put onto this plate of mine and whether I am gobbling them up without consideration. Right here, right now, I am going to make wiser choices in the management of my dinner plate, I have seen the banquet, and I know what I want. I will keep space available for my choices, and I will trust those around me to manage their own.

I am grateful for the knowledge that what I think is what I create. I will keep my mind full of hopeful thoughts, I will keep my heart full of love and peace. I will keep clear space on my plate. I will take baby steps towards where I want to be and I will harness whatever change I can influence.

April 14:

I am Love. I AM Love! I AM LOVE!!! I am grateful I realized it. Now to be brave and let that shine. I aspire to be unconditional Love. I'm not there yet, not by a long shot. I wonder how one can hold unconditional Love when there are unacceptable behaviours involved, how to separate the two? I appreciate it is not up to me to deem a behaviour as acceptable or unacceptable, but, I do have the right to identify the Energies I want to immerse myself in.

April 15:

My Little Roommates seem to be adjusting to this new communal living arrangement. I on the other hand am beginning to wonder why I ever thought this could possibly have been a good idea. I remind myself, my intentions were good. There must be something for me to learn in this. Perhaps many things. I am grateful for learning situations, and the resilience of My Little Roommates.

April 16:

At work I sit pre-dawn at the hotel front desk watching palm fronds wave in a frenzy through the atrium window. Cherry blossom branches ride the wind, bobbing up and down. Up and down. The early morning sky begins its transformation. Pockets of daybreak slowly appearing through varying degrees of grey.

April 17:

One of My Little Roommates got to celebrate her birthday with her friends and family in the city today. In nine years she hasn't had the opportunity to see both parents on her special day. I am grateful she had the opportunity. I am glad she felt how very loved and very cherished she is by so many people.

When I pick them up from the ferry and return home, the closer I get, the more physically ill I feel that we have to return to the slovenly belly of a hoarder's den.

"Oh" someone speaks up as I turn onto the road, "I forgot that we lived there."

Nothing was said after that sentiment. What could I say? There are no words I can offer.

April 18:

One on one birthday lunch moments with My Little Roommate and not a single bump on our interpersonal road today. When she was mid-metamorphosis from a baby to a toddler, I penned a little poem about the experience:

> She makes me laugh,
> she makes me cry,

> she makes me scratch my head
> and wonder why?

I smile at the beauty and bewilderment in our journey together. The poem still holds true. She is exquisitely fascinating and captivating. I am endlessly grateful.

April 19:

A friend visited our space today. I am grateful for someone to bear witness. To validate and empathize with my frustrations. I miss having an organized home environment. Life is not feeling terribly easy right now, but I am adamant there are still things to be grateful for. I am glad I reached out for support. I promise myself I will continue asking for support as often as I need to.

April 20:

The memories of my hikes before the move are beckoning me, inspiring me to venture out and discover new patches of forest to savour. I am grateful for the inclinations, and I am going to bump this higher up on my list of things to do. My life. My choice. My self-care. Take the time, so I don't end up serving time. It is entirely up to me how much I do, or don't, enjoy my own Life.

April 21:   FULL PINK MOON

★ FULL MOON REFLECTIONS:

- ○ HAVE I BEEN FEELING THE DESIRED EMOTIONS I IDENTIFIED IN MY NEW MOON INTENTIONS?

- ○ HAVE I BEEN TAKING TANGIBLE CONSISTENT ACTIONS IN THE DIRECTIONS OF MY HEART'S LONGING?

Continuing to struggle with angst, I have been focusing all of my Energy on clearing the six foot by six foot patch that will be my garden. This will be completed in time for planting season. Delay is non-negotiable.

I stood in that cleared patch of yard today and took my efforts underground like an archeological dig. Placing the shovel blade at the base of each stump, I hoist it, raising the root bulb to splice its tendrils below. Extracting the base, tracing the far reaching complex root system and yarding it out. For every inch of barbed vine that once stood here, it was matched by an inch of underground subconscious system that sustained it. As above, so below.

As I dig, the land finally spoke to me, whispering softly, oh so softly.... "*You are clearing me, and in return, I am clearing you.*"

April 22:

A couple of years ago I got lost in the woods with one of my daughters. As a rehabilitating city slicker whose only forest experiences were the likes of Stanley Park, I never appreciated how easily a trail in the bush can go unnoticed and one can become turned around. It wouldn't have been such a big deal, but we were lost and wandering for hours. She has Type 1 Diabetes and wears an insulin pump. In our hours trying to find our way back, all of her snacks were eaten and the juice boxes used to treat hypoglycaemia were being consumed far too quickly. I had to call authorities for assistance. Search and rescue was dispatched. It was a humbling and an embarrassing situation. The joke around our house is: it's a good thing my daughter was with me, I *had* to ask for help, otherwise, I'd stubbornly still be out there. There likely is some truth to that.

Clearly we were eventually found safely, but it was a traumatic enough experience that I become nervous exploring new sections of forest. Today, I bravely did. There came a point where I became confused as to direction, and I could feel panic begin to creep closer. *"I am not lost"* I spoke to myself aloud, repeating as necessary *"I am freestyling in the woods"*. I repeated that over and over as I finally got my bearings and got my dog and I back on the right trail again. *"I am freestyling, isn't this exciting?! Woohoo! Look at me... I am freestyling!"*

I am grateful I was able to shift *"lost in the woods"* to *"freestyling"* and managed to overcome anxiety. I promptly bought a new waterproof map of hiking trails and I am grateful!!! Making smart choices! Or trying to....

I am also grateful to not still be out there *"freestyling"*.

April 23:

Through a closed window and from a reasonable distance, I watch My Little Roommates trying to cooperate assembling a trampoline. I am grateful to recognize them *trying* to negotiate. I am so grateful to watch their personalities unfold. I am also especially grateful for closed windows and safe distances.

April 24:

The half moon is reminiscent of a button passing through its hole in the starry sky. A decreasing moon bears Energies of reduction and release. Of clearing and letting go. I stand in the yard, giving thanks to the sky and moon above. The time is upon me to consider what else in my life needs to be cleared and released.

April 25:

My symbolic conversations with a playful compassionate Universe continue. The latest symbol being the reappearance of keyhole shapes before me.

What am I unlocking? Continuing to collect clues, perhaps a key here or there to see if it fits... I hold a grateful heart.

April 26:

After much bumbling, fumbling, and cooperating with the co-tenant. Followed by some *more* bumbling and fumbling, a clenched jaw, some very intentional deep breaths and an internal pep talk with myself: my garden now has the beginning of a frame for plastic fencing. I very much need a space of my own. A place to tend to and grow. I am grateful to be exploring cooperative efforts. I am trying to release expectation. I am consciously choosing to listen and learn.

April 27:

Progress has been made! I have mounted two walls of the deer fencing so far. I am extra grateful for logistical lessons from previous gardens: build the raised beds and bring the soil in *before* fencing the entire perimeter. Better to be a slow learner than not to learn at all.

April 28:

Yesterday I found myself wearing my snarky pants. I tried to deflate it by identifying what was bothering me so much. Hoping to manage the situation, wanting to do no harm. Holding hope that whatever was bugging me would soon pass. But within minutes of waking, I found myself diving right back into my inventoried list of grievances.

Some days my mind does alright with minimal supervision. Other days, it's like being the zookeeper. I will not let that crap flinging Monkey Mind set the frequency of my thoughts. I am doing much *observing with detachment* and a lot of declarations of *"Oh, isn't that interesting".*

I am learning new ways.

April 29:

Headed into the garden for self-care today with the specific goal to mount plastic netting between the raised beams. Someone (who shall remain unidentified) followed close behind verbally processing their thoughts aloud. Setting the boundary, I clearly stated "I came into this corner of the yard to be by myself. I can't listen to you process aloud". Speaking my need calmly, clearly and with respect. Though despite my diplomacy it was quite evident feelings had been hurt.

As I learn to communicate my boundaries, I am learning to hold the space so as not to take on the emotional response of another. I am learning new ways. I am practicing new skills. I am grateful.

April 30:

All of my control freak issues have RSVP'd to this party. ALL OF THEM. Which has been an epiphany in itself: how did I not *recognize* my controlling behaviour? Until this week, I thought I was a fairly easy going person. Able to compromise. Work as part of the team. I need a minute to recover from the laughter in my head.

Martyrdom comes in many different forms. I am learning that when I don't feel control, I martyr myself. Holy ding-a-ding-a-ling light bulb moment! How did I not see that before now? Suddenly the angst I have been experiencing the last few days all makes sense. I plunged myself into a communal cohabitation. I am no longer reigning supreme.

I remind myself and repeat as necessary: "I am releasing all expectations and all outdated attitudes of limitation. For the Highest Good of All." I am grateful for the opportunities to implement lessons I am currently learning.

May
2016

"AM I MAKING THIS HARDER FOR MYSELF?"

May 1:

I tied together the layers of plastic fencing that defines the perimeter of my garden. Each twine knot is tied with a prayer; a blessing for Mother Earth and all her inhabitants. When I am finished tying the prayer knots I tie lengths of ribbon to each wall of the netting. The colours of the ribbon matching each direction and corresponding element: North (Earth) green and brown. East (Air) has white and light blue. South (Fire) yellow, red and orange. West (Water) blue, purple and green.. I've written wishes along the ribbons and imagine hopes riding the wind. Scattering with the breeze and taking hold like wildflower seeds, eventually germinating and blossoming. Magick is in the air, and I am grateful.

May 2:

I am confused. I am frustrated. I have recognized the futility in over investing my Energy in helping someone. It's one thing to take someone's hand, approach the dance floor together, and participate in a cooperative choreography. It is a *very* different experience taking a lever trying to wedge a boulder out of place and hoping it will dance. I am learning precisely how effective a distraction this is. One more subconscious act of self-sabotage.

Despite my increasing frustration and dwindling respect, I am grateful to be modelling peaceful co-existence. There is no need for drama in this situation. So I bite my tongue. Pick my battles. Choose my words carefully. Opt to reinvest Energy into myself and my dreams.

May 3:

I am grateful for a stretch of four days off work. Thai take out on the beach, me myself and I. Solitude. In this extremely challenging period I recognize self-care as a crucial priority. I am grateful for this hard earned wisdom.

May 4:

I am grateful for a happy, healthy, sweet natured dog. Bless her heart for trying to be low maintenance despite her lack of understanding personal space. She would be happiest if I could find a baby carrier and strap all sixty pounds of her to me. She'd be thrilled to be constantly held and get to see everyone eye to eye. I am grateful to know her clingy love, even when I joke that it is the kind of love that feels like you're being strangled.

May 5:

I am grateful for the little things. Chamomile scattered throughout the lawn. Tall foxgloves swaying back and forth in Spring winds.

May 6:   *NEW MOON*

★ NEW MOON. NEW CYCLE. NEW INTENTIONS:

- WHAT INTENTION AM I SETTING FOR THIS NEXT LUNAR CYCLE?
- HOW DO I WANT TO FEEL THROUGHOUT THIS MONTH?
- WHAT DO I WANT TO SET INTO ACTION: WHAT DO I WANT TO ACCOMPLISH?
- AM I HARNESSING MY OWN ENERGIES AND INVESTING THEM WISELY?

I want to reconnect with my own priorities. I am no longer interested in hooking into crazy making. I remind myself all of this is happening *around* me... I am not in it. I breathe. I ground and centre. Inhaling deeply. Imagining tree roots emerging from the arches of my feet, spreading from the tips of my toes, spreading, expanding, far reaching through the dirt of Mother Earth below. Anchoring me.

I call upon my Higher Self, all of my Angels, Messengers and Spirit Guides. Aid me in redirecting my Energies into myself and my dreams. Assist me in not buying into drama, for that matter, not *creating* drama. Help reinforce my mindfulness and self-awareness, so I may recognize patterns I am subconsciously partaking in.

I planted my seeds in the garden today. When I dropped them into tiny mounds of fertile soil, I imagined my intentions being planted alongside. I tuck them in gently, lovingly. Giving thanks for all that they will grow into and the future abundance they will yield.

Burying them in the dark moist soil, I have total trust and faith they will germinate on their own accord. I will not dig them up to ensure they are doing as they should. Nor shall I do that in my Life. I have planted the seeds and I shall focus on holding trust.

I give thanks to the North, the East, the South, and the West. I give thanks to the Above, and I give thanks to the Below. I give thanks to the Within, and I give thanks to the Without. I give thanks to Mother Father Creator and an All compassionate All providing Universe. Thank you Mother Moon, unseen above in your total darkness. Thank you for watching over us all. I give deep thanks to all of the Angels and Light Beings working to reinforce the cosmic grid of Light that holds our Mother Earth. Thank you. Thank you. Thank you. Thank you for this Life lived thus far. Thank you for all the learning via moments of contrast. Thank you for aiding in this magnificent unfolding.

I will breathe. I will trust. I will cha cha cha.

May 7:

I bought a variety of new sage plants today and tucked them lovingly into a planter box.

Somewhere in the sky, high above beyond my own sight, is the faintest sliver of a waxing crescent moon that has embarked on its gradual transition into fullness. I do not need to see it to know that it is there. It is growing. It is transforming. I give thanks, I trust.

Daylight hours are stretching longer and longer. Dwindling dusk arrived tonight at 8:55pm. We are nearing the peak of summer. The cycle continues in its constant spiral. I am grateful for natural rhythms and surrendering to flow. All is unfolding just as it should, in its own innate timing. Just as it always does.

May 8:

Today was a beautiful sunny day and I was able to clean the kitchen with all the doors and windows open. Welcoming fresh air into the house in an effort to combat the odor of motorcycle grease and decades of decaying papers stacked in towers of cardboard boxes.

I would sage the kitchen area but this Energy is beyond anything I can influence. It saddens me I have to prepare my family's meals in the midst of this. I realize how limited I am in managing and influencing the Energy of the shared space and choose to harness what I am able to influence, focusing my domestic magick for the privacy of our own quarters.

Twisting and turning. Twisting and turning. Twisting and turning my soulful kaleidoscope to rediscover gratitude.

Repeating again for my own reference: *I am grateful it was a beautiful sunny day and I had the opportunity to clean with all the doors and windows open.*

May 9:

Two months into this new living arrangement and part of me whispers remorsefully, *"What have I done? What have I done?"*

I remember my life strategist commenting in session more than a year ago, on weird ways she had seen her clients self-sabotage when progress was beginning to be made, because somewhere they held the subconscious belief that they did not deserve to pursue their Life calling. Had she somehow intuited I would throw myself under the bus?

Recognizing what I have done here, I claim radical responsibility in how I created this situation. Uncertain of the future. Impatient with the development of progress, I took drastic action. As a result, I certainly made *something* happen.

Can't help but wonder what would have happened if I *hadn't* listened to whispers of Intuition. But with exorbitant costs of living, I don't know that it would have been any more beneficial of a situation. Once again, I spiral back to trust: something will become of this strange situation. Whether it be a lesson. Mine... or another's. Perhaps I am sifting and sorting, releasing all that no longer serves.

"Are you still there, Kali-Ma? Is this still part of the destruction and rebirth?"

I cannot have it both ways. I cannot be willing, yet be regretful. There is no half in, half out. The only way out is through. I give thanks I am becoming clearer, even if right now, it's about as clear as mud. I shall rise forth and bloom like a lotus.

Turning to my Angels and Spirit Guides, I ask for assistance, *"Help me. Help me not be swayed or bogged down by circumstances, my own hopeful expectations, or the emotions around me. Higher Self, please help me rise above: if only for today."*

I am learning big lessons. Huge lessons. Epic lessons. I am grateful for them all.

May 10:

Accepting I cannot change anyone other than myself, I am not interested in imposing my expectations on another.

That being said, I have full responsibility as to the Energies I immerse my family in. This living arrangement is impacting my peace of mind and quality of life. I admit that I moved us into a situation that does not serve. Since I am not prepared to accept life on these terms, I have informed the co-tenant it is my intention to move. However, we live in an isolated part of the province and a popular summertime tourist destination. The reality of finding an *affordable* pet friendly long term rental just before summer is unlikely.

I am grateful to be reuniting with my creativity, my spirituality, my power, my magickal essence. I am turning to my creativity more and more as a means of coping and healthy escape from the cluttered chaos of this environment.

May 14:

Grateful for a sleeping dog stretched across the length of my bed. My Little Roommates are in the city visiting DaddyMan. I have created artificial silence with earplugs, time, space and solitude in our attic for creative expression whilst the co-tenant mutters, putters, belches and farts from his floor. I am learning so much this year about holding space.

May 15:

Upon collecting My Little Roommates, I offer them a heartfelt apology, admitting that I cannot maintain my well being in that cabin. We are going to have to move. I express my concern that we may not be able to find a rental home over the summer months, but if we can persevere, if we can practice patience and hold hope, I will get us out of this situation. I *refuse* to create an environment of imposed secrecy; I go home and notify the co-tenant of my intentions.

I am not fond of the taste of defeat. I will not judge or criticize myself. I will focus on finding compassion for myself and for all involved.

May 16:

I am grateful for a dog's big sleepy golden eyes staring up at me over the blankets of an unmade bed.

May 17:

Inspired by a friend's joyful rediscovery of nature where she is staying, I am deliberately getting us out and immersing us in nature. When My Little Roommates were at school today, I had the opportunity and privilege to visit two beaches today. Time and space to myself, beachcombing and listening to waves crash. Thank you Mother Nature.

May 18:

My Little Roommates have excitedly begun their countdown to summer break from school. I am grateful for the possibility of summer days spent in the forest and the beaches.

May 19:

After venturing into town and connecting with me after my shift, one of My Little Roommates declares, "I'm glad you work each Sunday. It gives us the chance to be free range!"

I am grateful for the transition of unfolding independence.

May 20:

"I sure am happy to be sharing attic space with you," My Little Roommate declares. My heart melts.

May 21:   **FULL FLOWER MOON**

★ FULL MOON REFLECTIONS:

- ○ HAVE THE EMOTIONS I'VE BEEN EXPERIENCING BEEN ALIGNED WITH MY NEW MOON INTENTIONS?
- ○ AM I HOLDING HOPE OR AM I FOCUSING ON LACK?
- ○ WHAT ACTIONS HAVE I TAKEN TOWARDS WHAT I WANT TO BUILD, CREATE, AND GROW?
- ○ AM I EMBRACING FLOW OR AM I MAKING THINGS HARDER AND MORE COMPLICATED?

My intentions were to refocus on my priorities. Trusting that all is unfolding just as it needs to. Not hooking into drama or distraction. I have accepted that I will not tolerate a life such as this, and that I have the power to remove myself from this situation. I have made committed efforts towards my self-care. I breathe... I trust... I cha cha cha.

Tonight I am grateful for the tiny birds that swoop past the big windows on the main level towards their nests and bird houses. Whoops! One of them just flew directly into the window with a thunk. I know that feeling little bird, know that feeling.

May 22:

As I toil in the garden dog charges from the yard. Bolting off in pursuit of shadows in the forest. I am grateful she returns willingly when I call her. Returning my focus to the garden bed, I envision pulling my own mental weeds. Weeds of over-investing, martyrdom and stubborn adamancy I can still make this situation work. I pull. I clear. I monitor. I give thanks.

May 23:

I am grateful I have once again stopped smoking cigarettes. Again. Seriously, you'd think I'd remember how much fun this quitting process is and stop picking one up. I will continue to keep away from them despite a stressful environment and sharing the property with a smoker. I look forward to the day I can have my windows open without cigarette smoke wafting in.

May 24:

I had begun a large acrylic painting before we moved. A 24 x 30 canvas of Lakshmi the Hindu Goddess of prosperity and abundance. I made a conscious point of reconnecting with the her today. My venomous Inner Critic was strangely silent as I practice observing the painting's unfolding with a freeing blend of detachment and playful curiosity. I am grateful for a peaceful mind and side stepping my own self-judgement.

May 25:

Observations from the forest: With my focus set on the trail before me, I don't appreciate the breathtaking beauty of what I am walking through, until I have doubled back and am experiencing the opposite approach.

I am grateful for lush moss in the deep shade of the forest, and the ancient wisdoms that ride the wind whispering to me.

May 26:

I got my garlic planted today. I would have rather had it planted last autumn, but I wasn't here and the garden didn't exist. I don't judge. It is what it is and it's not what it's not. I planted garlic today and for that I will choose gratitude.

I went for a long walk with one of My Little Roommates today, and was intrigued by a notice printed on bright fluorescent pink paper posted on a community bulletin board. It was an advertisement for an intuitive mediumship workshop. I went home and registered.

Normally, it isn't something that I would particularly do. But I am practising stretching this year, doing different things and trying new experiences. I am grateful for the opportunity and for community bulletin boards.

That which I seek is also seeking me.

May 27:

I am grateful I seized this strange opportunity. As stated before, I had hoped it would serve the Highest Good of All parties involved. I now have to release that hope and subsequent disappointment. I give myself permission to remove us from a situation that does not serve our well-being. I turn to my Angels, my Messengers and my Spirit Guides. I turn to my 'Beloved I Am Presence': *"Help me hold compassion for all involved."*

May 28:

I am grateful for this morning's sight of a cruise ship on the ocean horizon as I turn out of the driveway. I send Love Bubbles to all on board and wish them all a fabulous vacation experience!

Dear eyes: thank you for all you do for me.

May 29:

Both My Little Roommates had momentous milestones of independence today. One had their first independent trip on public transit. The other began a part time job. They are growing up. I am grateful to bear witness to their journeys.

May 30:

Grateful for blossoms cascading down in a swirled descent upon a Spring storm. Grateful for the sight of petals stuck in puddles along the edge of the winding road.

May 31:

The rental section of the classifieds horrifies me. First with its two whopping advertisements, then with the exorbitant rents being asked. Knowing we are going to be moving at some point, I am sticking to a strict budget and an accompanying meal plan, saving everything I can for moving expenses. I hope it will be sooner rather than later. I have a choice here: I can focus on the worrying about lack of availability, or I can hold gratitude for making conscientious financial choices. I am choosing to focus on the gratitude. I know what I focus on is fed and increased by my Energy. I am not interested in creating more worry for myself. I am grateful for this awareness of Universal Law.

June
2016

"SHIFTING STORIES
AND
RAISING VIBRATIONS"

June 1:

I am shifting my money story. Shedding some very outdated, poverty mentality beliefs. I now choose to recognize money as nothing more than one of many different forms of Energy. An Energy that flows as long as not obstructed. I am open to receiving and sharing within this flow of exchange and abundance.

June 2:

All of the rentals advertised are Air B&B's. I whisper to myself *"that which I seek is also seeking me"*. I am choosing to hold gratitude and hope, refusing to allow myself to fret. When I feel myself clenching about it: I forgive myself and release.

June 3:

With such limited advertised rental housing I'm generating as much word of mouth amongst my community as I can. Anyone that knows me, knows that I need to find a rental house. My search is regularly being posted publicly on my Facebook status and I'm grateful for the many community members that are sharing it within their networks. I have created a bright, artful poster with a bold headline *"Have you seen our home?"* highlighting my budget and describing our needs. I will begin distributing them on tomorrow's New Moon.

I opt not to focus on my frustration, intentionally redirecting my perspective to all that I have to be grateful for. There are always blessings, and I refuse to lose sight of that.

June 4:   *NEW MOON*

★ New Moon. New Cycle. New Energies. New Intentions:

- How do I want to feel throughout the next lunar cycle?

- WHERE DO I WANT TO GROW?
- WHAT *WILL* I DO TO SUPPORT MY EXPANSION?

As I plant zucchini and more lettuce seeds this afternoon, I plant imagined seeds of permission alongside. Permission to freely and honestly communicate my needs. I plant the intention to get out of my own way. I plant seeds for honest self-awareness. A tiny spider scurries. A leaf overhead falls, twirling as though dancing in its descent.

Thank you Mother Father Creator.
Thank you my 'Beloved I Am Presence'.
I will be brave.
I **am** brave.

June 5:

One of My Little Roommates says, "Remember when we went back to the old house, and all the magick was gone and deflated? It's us! It's us! We're the magick!"

I am grateful for enchanted childhood observations. Consequently I have dubbed our space "The Magick Attick". My affectionate pet name is two fold: first, to honour our mystical nature. Secondly, to better contain our separate space, to work with the Energy contained within.

Long may it be the power of three: grateful, grateful, grateful.

June 6:

I am grateful for paint on my hands before going to bed. I am grateful for electricity, clean running water, a roof and walls that keep out wind and rain.

June 7:

I am grateful for moored sailboats softly swaying on the ocean waves, swaying back and forth, back and forth, like a metronome on the slowest of settings.

June 8:

I have been battling my abusive Inner Critic and the scat flinging organ grinding Monkey Mind all of my life. In January when I committed to myself I would share no more fragmented offerings, I had a lot of "*who do you think you are?*" venomously being spewed through my brain. I also had great trepidation because I know that what I am here to express and to share is not yet mainstream culture. It is considered "woowoo" (which I will get back to in a moment). My sidestep trickster response to the cruelty going on in my brain, was to create and express under a sort of nom de plume, the Grateful Goblin.

Years ago a friend of mine dubbed me Goblin for when my mind recklessly unleashed a barrage of cruelty upon myself. I used to be my own greatest enemy. In time I learned to use gratitude as my life saving device to combat the Goblin's reign of terror.

I used the name as a camouflaged shield to express and speak honestly about subject matters that for so long many insisted I shouldn't talk about. Grateful Goblin spoke to the duality of my human experience, it spoke of a struggle to love, accept and find peace within myself. The name also helped me find my audience and tribe. If you could get on board with the Grateful Goblin, then you would be okay when I started talking about magick, alchemy and Universal Law.

Back to woowoo for a moment. I have some very mixed feelings about the term being used to describe new age or unconventional spirituality. Now granted it is a very effective disclaimer. When you say woowoo people have a sense of what is coming. But, that being said, it is remarkably invalidating and cloaked with disrespect. We are not woowoo. We are Lightworkers. We are facilitating a shift in consciousness and the world is waiting for us to share our Light with our communities. When I get out of my own way and share my offering, it gives you permission to do the same, and when you do the same, it gives your neighbour permission as well. Not that permission is necessary, but it creates the space and the possibility.

I am not woowoo. I am magick. You are too. There just seems to be a lot of people resisting their inherent magickal abilities. That's okay. For now. They will wake up on their own time according to the Law of Cycles. But perhaps... just perhaps your awakening will vibrate in their direction and the ripple effect will facilitate the stirring. Let us not distract ourselves with the Light of those around us for now, let us tend to our own magickal hearths and stoke the flame to a roaring blaze. They will see the Light and they will feel the warmth.

Today I am deeply grateful for the progress I have made in being brave enough to share the Grateful Goblin. I am at a progress checkpoint, and I am looking back at how far I have come.

June 9:

After an hour's drive from home, I visited her today, that dear old friend that I visited every day for hours all through Winter. My confidant, my muse, my therapist... sometimes, my Magic 8 Ball. Today, I visited my favourite beloved patch of Pender Harbour forest.

Having only known time with her in late Autumn and Winter, and having been absent from her graces all Spring, I was surprised today by her lush fullness. Walking in to greet her, it felt as though a loved one was wrapping their arms around me, and I cried. Actually, I was intrigued by how *much* I cried, but opted to let tears flow without judgement. Offering teardrops to the forest floor below as I walked deeper and deeper into the woods.

So many changes had been contemplated here and I was hoping she would have answers for me again today. They didn't come readily. So I continued in silence as I walked along an overgrown trail, passing into what now is a full meadow abundant with wildflowers. I hiked for hours, my happy canine girl and I, and nothing was coming.

I began thinking about where I was in life when I last visited my beloved forest Goddess. Reflecting on the changes, the sudden and gargantuan leaps I had made this year. My heart began to sag heavy beneath the weight of burdened doubt as I considered whether the changes had been to my detriment while benefitting those around me. Had this been another example of subconscious self-sacrifice? In my mind I could begin to hear the mechanical wind up tunes of that old menacing organ grinder, and though I couldn't see that Monkey Mind, I could smell the pungent poop hanging thick in the air. Outdated stories of limitation and antiquated self flagellating stories of worthlessness whirled around my brain.

As the mental angst began gaining strength, this was my sink or swim moment. To either tame the thought process or to allow a torrential tornado to reign down upon me. I began looking for something to be grateful for, and in that moment of harnessing my mentalism, that beloved forest Goddess fleetingly whispered to me before quickly disappearing again amongst green leaves and wildflowers swaying in the wind..... *"We are in flux"*.

We are in flux. When I think of that sentence, I see a towel that is being wrung out. We are in flux, and it is important, *it is crucial*, that we remain open and flexible to what happens next. Flexibility and openness is paramount.

On my drive back home a church sign along the roadside read "May our hopes, not our hurts, shape our future". Indeed. May I recognize when the organ grinding Monkey Mind begins spewing ugly old songs and dances. May I then, instead, opt to raise hope into the Summer sky like a kite. Giving a little extra string allowing winds of possibility to carry it higher.

That which I seek is also seeking me.

I am grateful.

June 10:

For years I have loved making ransom note style collages, forming sentences with letters cut from magazines pasted together. Old school cut and paste. Despite the utter joy it brings me, I have judged it and been nearly ashamed of it.

"That's so stupid. That's not art. It requires no talent. A kid in kindergarten could do that! No one is going to appreciate that".

I only shared it with a select few whom I thought might appreciate it. I used to be so busy criticizing myself that I didn't dare to allow others to see me for fear that they would compound my internal angst with their own critiques and criticisms.

I have finally realized it's not up to me to narrowly share my creative offerings. My only job is to get out of my own way and be open to expressing it. They don't like it? That's okay. I will survive. My creativity is my return offering, my tithing if you will, to my Mother Father Creator, the all compassionate, all providing, all loving Universe. The audience is not in it. It is between me and my Creator.

Tonight, I am grateful for this liberating realization regarding my unique collage style. I am finally learning to get out of my own way. Deeply, deeply grateful.

June 11:

Today I attended the intuitive medium workshop I synchronistically found the advertisement for.

I went to a nearby restaurant by myself on the lunch break. While waiting for my order to arrive, I was invited to join another group of participants at their table. Moving beyond social anxiety, I opted to do something different again and accepted the invitation. Not saying much, I observe, listening to the conversation around me. I must have zoned out into a kind of softened gaze; one of the established and reputable intuitives in the group turns to me and asks, "Do you read people naturally?" Caught off guard, all I knew was I had been checking in. Sensing whether I felt comfortable, or safe, around these new acquaintances. What she had asked me helped me to realize that is *exactly* what I was doing. I had never realized it! I have done this all my life; sensing whether or not I felt safe. Like a snake smelling the air with its tongue discerning if there was any concern. I always figured it was just a survivor thing. Her question didn't just bring it to my attention, she validated what I was doing was genuine.

Just like that, another piece of the puzzle clicked into place. Awestruck with deep gratitude. I learned something new about myself today! My mysterious unfolding continues.

June 12:

"My body is healthy, my mind is brilliant, my Spirit is calm... I am grateful".

Today I birthed one of those ransom note style collages reading these exact words. I cannot describe how the selecting, the cutting, the pasting is absolute play for me. What a treat to have the opportunity to indulge. Aaaaah, play is some powerful medicine!

June 13:

I observed today that my garden is the greenest and I have been the more creative than ever in a mere three months after a move. Talk about coping mechanisms!

A part of me sheepishly recognizes that coping mechanisms wouldn't be necessary if I wasn't as stressed by the physical conditions of the house we share. In a strange way this chaotic environment is scraping me raw. Opening me into a bloody weeping wound. Allowing the opportunity for me to choose my own healing medicine. When the healing is done and behind me the scar will be strong new flesh. Perhaps the time has come to become grateful for all of it.

Can I do that? More accurately will I allow myself to do that? I breathe and I trust and I sit with this new realization.

June 14:

"I love you".... My Little Roommate replies "I love me too!". Yes, yes, yes!!!! A beaming smile spreads across my face like the sunrise and my heart lets loose a happy dance of gratitude.

June 15:

Today I had a very candid and mature conversation with the co-tenant. Nothing has changed regarding the cluttered chaotic environment in the cabin. My plans to vacate remain the same as soon as a rental vacancy presents itself. There is no point in creating drama, getting uppity or angry while we remain living here waiting in transition. It serves no benefit and would only make everything that much more difficult. I am grateful for maturity, peace and diplomacy.

June 16:

I am continuing to stretch beyond my comfort zone by sharing my creative offerings as the Grateful Goblin. Representing myself as such at a social mixer hosted tonight by the life strategist I've been working with. 'Stretch' doesn't seem to effectively express my level of discomfort. I am working through a strange enigmatic paradox of yearning to be seen, yet at the same time not *wanting* to be seen. The vulnerability and inner conflict over this internal tug of war has been fascinating to observe.

There are two responses to introducing yourself to someone new as the Grateful Goblin. The first, and most common reception, is a sort of scrunched up *"that's weird"* expression. The second, and far less common reception, is a lit up expression full of intrigue. I am learning to hold the space and observe the first response as comical. People are entitled to their reactions. It's got nothing to do with me. I'm not in that. I am grateful for this profound happy learning.

I donated two door prizes for tonight's social mixer: a collaged found font affirmation canvas and a full size poster I created of this year's moon phases. My body grew rigid with tension; the taste of rising bile heavy upon my tongue when the door prizes were being announced. My body was in fight or flight mode and believe you me, all I wanted to do was flee! In a room of what felt like a hundred women, there was no way bursting into tears and running from the room would go unnoticed. I had to pull up my big girl pants. Launching into an internal pep talk I held my ground, convincing myself that my wedgie clenched expression presented as a confident toothy smile.

Smile Goblin, smile. Breathe Goblin, breathe. You've got this. Ooops, we may want to add control your bladder to this list. A urine soaked Goblin is a tough sell. Smile. Breathe. Maintain composure.

I am grateful I moved through such an intense moment of anxiety. I am learning new ways. I am doing things differently.

June 17:

Still no advertised homes for rent. I am spreading the word to friends, acquaintances and basically anyone I meet, that my family is seeking a home to rent on a long term basis. I am grateful that when I caught myself exploding with anxiety, I breathed through it, contained my Energy, and didn't do anything impulsive.

I deliberately visited the forest this afternoon for self-care. Therapeutic medicine for this trying period. An unseen raven cries from above as I gaze at long tufts of moss hanging from overhead branches. The intoxicating smell of wet forest fills my lungs and feeds my Soul. Dog and I descend along the edge of a raised embankment that follows a rushing creek below. When we reach the clearing at the bottom, I crouch down to cup rushing water to quench my thirst.

Walking back I consider the many different ways I've recreated previous dysfunctional dynamics by believing the things that I think. Especially in my relationships. If I continue walking around telling myself I am being judged I am going to continue feeling judged.

First I have to stop believing what I am thinking. Then I am going to shift my thoughts to another mindset. I am going to stop repeating bullshit stories to myself! Right here, right now, beginning today: I give myself permission to be who I truly am! I am strong. I am skilled. I am educated. I am self-aware. I am loving and compassionate. I am worthy of being respected. I have done remarkably well in learning to set boundaries and I will continue to practice being non-reactive with others. I am Love. I am Light. I am a magickal conduit. I am the Universe wrapped in skin having a human experience.

I am deeply grateful.

June 18:

I am grateful for a child-free Saturday. Everyone is gone and I can cook in the kitchen in peace, silence and solitude. I set up a temporary altar space on the windowsill so I have something to focus on other than the chaos of the kitchen. The shrine includes a framed drawing of Ganesh (the Hindu deity of overcoming obstacles), a selection of crystals, a statue of Sarasvati. (The Hindu Goddess of music, poetry and knowledge.) The window is open a crack and I savour the sound of falling rain. Focusing on infusing my stovetop creations with Love and Light for whom I shall share the nourishment.

June 19:

My Little Roommate scrambles up the length of my body wrapping me tightly in a hug upon her return home. Her arms gripping me. Legs entwined around my hips. I am grateful for easy loving affection.

What an *honour* to be loved that much!

June 20:   FULL STRAWBERRY MOON
                                              SUMMER SOLSTICE

Winter Solstice has the least amount of daylight hours in a twenty four hour period and Summer Solstice has the polar opposite. This is a powerful day. Fruits are ripening, growing that much closer to harvesting. In order to honour and harness the Energies of this powerful ancient day, I broaden my full moon introspection. Reflecting on *everything* that has transpired since Winter Solstice. There have been some deep powerful pivotal points of transformation and change thus far.

I have been brave. I am grateful.

I have navigated winds of change. I am grateful.

I have become clear on what will work and what will not. I am grateful.

I have become clear as to who I wish to be, and who I can shed. I am grateful.

I am becoming a Soul more brave, more daring, more beautiful and intriguing than I ever could've dreamt or imagined!

Thank you Mother Father Creator. Thank you my 'Beloved I Am Presence'. Thank you Grateful and Thank you Goblin. I hold awe for a moment. I celebrate all that I have ever survived, and all that I will ever come to experience. Deep. Deep. Deep thanks.

I am grateful for a thriving garden and the peaceful patch amidst the cluttered chaos of the property. I am grateful to have created such a beautiful sanctuary. The co-tenant asks me, "Did you plant fringed poppies beneath the window?" declaring in disbelief and surprise, "I've never seen them there before". We hadn't. They just sprung up. More evidence of the magick that flows in the wake of My Little Roommates and I.

With this change of seasons, I vow to myself I will honour my own cycle of growth. I am surrendering my resistance and I now choose to allow the unfolding of my Highest Calling. Like the root system of the prickled thicket in the backyard that I cleared months ago, I now release all that inhibits or prevents progression.

June 21:

The moon is beginning to reduce from its visible ripe fullness. It is time for me to likewise release and harness powerful rhythms and change. What can I now release, that has not been serving the Highest Good of All?

The kitchen. The communal shared kitchen. It is causing such turmoil and sadness. It is time to release.

No longer will I try to make that kitchen scenario work. No longer will I share that refrigerator. No longer will I feed my children amongst towers of cardboard boxes, and act like it is perfectly normal.

No more!

I'm done!!

I will no longer leak my Energy grumbling about what I cannot change. Instead I now choose to deliberately harness what influence I *do* have.

There is a counter with a kitchen sink and cabinets along the far basement wall that is one of My Little Roommate's bedroom space. She has hated having that in her bedroom area since day one. Before encroaching on her space I turn to her for her blessing, "Can I set up our own kitchen area down here?" When she agrees we rearrange the long room using a large bookshelf to divide her bedroom area from what is going to become our kitchen. A mini bar fridge up in the Magick Attick that houses juice boxes to treat low blood sugars is lugged down two steep flights of stairs relocating it next to the basement counter. With the purchase of a dual electric hot plate we have created our own "Girls Cafe".

When I cannot change what is around me, *I harness what change I can.* I am grateful for this wisdom and resourcefulness.

June 22:

When I have misplaced something such as my coffee, car keys, or purse- I call it aloud, like I'm calling a pet: "Coffee!?"... "Cofffffeeeeeeee"......"Cooooooooffffffffffffeeeeeeeeee".

It drives My Little Roommates nuts, but regardless, the misplaced item always seems to appear within a matter of moments.

I figure if it works on conjuring car keys, it can work on a home too. I have taken to driving around town with My Little Roommates, playfully calling out through open car windows "Home!? Hooooommmmmmmeeeeee!?"

That which we seek is also seeking us. We hope to meet it soon.

June 23:

Two snake sightings today on the trail. One of which was curled up on a bed of moss basking in the sun as if it were a little nest. I remind myself a snake does not look back mournfully at skin she has shed. She keeps slithering onward.

Thank you Universe for these symbolic messages. I am listening. I am hopeful. I trust I am being redirected. I breathe…. I trust… I cha cha cha.

June 24:

Driving along the forest access road to where I have been hiking with dog as of late, seven turkey vultures rise into flight from tall grasses. Their huge wing span opening up amongst the morning mist. My Little Roommate and I gasp at the sudden expansive sight.

This strange cohabitation scenario has been so draining. As of late I've observed my Inner Victim mentality wants me to just give up. She is ready to assume the fetal position and wither away in this cabin of cardboard boxes. She wants to relinquish all of our personal power. This is no prison. We are not hostages being held against our will. This is not a hunger strike in which she can lay our personal power on the metal meal tray and slide it in refusal through the passage slot of an imagined prison cell. She conveniently forgets that I got us into this situation willingly.

"Ahem!" I clear my throat calling her attention to my voice. *"That is NOT yours to give away!"* I scoop our personal power back up from her untouched meal tray and place it carefully into a medicine pouch I carry close to my heart.

Between the Inner Critic, the organ grinding Monkey Mind and now the Inner Victim joining the fray it's been a full time job trying not to be pulled into their mindsets. To observe what is going on in my head with detachment. Refusing to engage in it, raising my eyebrows, perhaps rolling my eyes, and once again repeating, *"isn't that interesting".*

I know that relinquishing my personal power is the threshold to perpetuating a sense of martyred victimhood.

I no longer do the tumultuous tango of asking, "*Why do I do this?*". "*Why?*" just sends me tumbling down the rabbit hole of distraction. It is what it is. It is appearing so I may release it as it no longer serves. I shall strive to hold no judgement, cast no criticism, no shame, just offer a heartfelt ***"isn't that interesting".***

By now knowing better I can do better. I can respond differently, can shift and transmute it.

Beginning by confiscating the refused meal tray out of the Victim's hands I sternly announce with great confidence to all the characters in my mind, I am the exclusive holder of my own power. They need not worry. They need not act up. I got this. I own how I got myself here, and now I will be accountable and navigate how I respond. What I think, I create, and I *have* the power to get us out of this. It begins with practicing patience and holding the vision. I *must* hold the vision.

Since I've reclaimed the pouch of personal power from the Victim's clenches, I think it's time to confiscate the megaphone from the Inner Critic. Pry the organ grinder away from the Monkey Mind's nimble fingers.

"I got this"

I breathe.... I trust.... I cha cha cha.

June 25:

I am nervous about My Little Roommates' emotional well being in the cabin's chaos over summer vacation when I am at work. I encourage them to go outside. To scramble up the exquisite climbing tree next to my garden, to explore the forest surrounding the property. I am grateful we are in an area where after a ten minute walk they can access public transit. I hold hope this surreal scenario will result in a new found sense of independence.

June 26:

In this strained cluttered cohabitation it is too easy for us to become angry out of frustration. Too easy to succumb to judgement instead of practicing compassion. I am too stubborn to allow us to be dragged down into emotional misery by this. This will **not** be the theme of our remaining chapters for the three of us.

In response to our unhappiness I am mindfully determined to initiate joyous experiences that will lift the spirits of my daughters and I. We spend a lot of our days driving to the opposite end of the coast to our favourite swimming lake. Using happy activities as a hopeful floatation device for us to hang onto when we return to the cluttered chaotic reality of the cabin.

Universal Law of Vibration: what we vibrate we will attract more of. By deliberately putting us in a happier state of mind I am raising our vibration.

Driving back from the lake I am calling "home" again aloud. My Little Roommate requests, "Let's roll up the window so not everyone hears you calling home".

"But there's no one around to hear".

"It's okay," she retorts reassuringly, "the houses out here have good ears. They know".

June 27:

One of My Little Roommates got to reconnect and channel her Inner Wolf Cub this afternoon. Her four paws completely submerged along the banks of Crystal Creek. Her rear end and imaginary tail high in the air, gulping fresh glacier run off. Her hair fans upon the water's surface around her. I am honoured to witness this moment of her pure wild. Thrilled to have this one on one time with her in the forest.

My other Little Roommate, the detail oriented planner, is coordinating dates with her flock of friends. I am amazed how personalities so stark in contrast can emerge from the same gene pool. One, ruminating over every conceivable detail, the other entrenched in imaginative daydreams as she leaps from rock to rock.

I am grateful for my yin and yang daughters, creating the *whole* of my parenting experience. I never knew unconditional love until I gave birth to these children. They are the thumpity thump thump of my beating heart walking around outside of my body.

June 28:

Walking across the hotel parking lot at 5:45am to start my shift, the waning half moon hangs overhead, beaming softly. I love being greeted by her in the early mornings.

June 29:

When you are feeding a family of three out of a mini bar fridge you shop daily. Before pulling the car into a parking spot I remark to My Little Roommates, "Nope- wrong store". At which point we drove 15-20 minutes to the next grocery store. Where I was delighted to bump into two very charming Souls I had not seen for quite some time. I am grateful I listened to my Intuition and for the synchronistic chats that unfolded.

June 30:

We drove an hour to our favourite lake again today. Being disheartened by the physical environment of where we are staying, I am determined to seek out and create happy experiences. Basking on the lake's embankment, we meet two new acquaintances: another mother and her adult daughter. They are quickly smitten over my dog's ridiculous stick retrieving water antics. Sharing remorsefully that they recently had to euthanize their beloved dog of the same breed. Our dog comforted two bruised hearts this afternoon. Filled their love tanks. It was a delight to witness the interactions. I am grateful.

July
2016

"TRANSITION
AND
SPARKS OF INSPIRATION"

July 1:

House magick. I dusted, swept, and vacuumed the Magick Attick today. I am grateful for the opportunity to sage and work with the Energy within our separate space. Thank heavens for separate spaces free from towers of cardboard boxes.

I am grateful for the smell of burning sage, cedar and sweetgrass.

July 2:

I am grateful for hiking with dog. The slugs, the snakes, and the snails on the trail. On our way out from the mouth of the forest a screech owl sweeps towards the treetops clenching a garter snake in its talons. I was surprised to see the owl during the day, and to see it with its prey dramatically dangling beneath it was an amazing sight.

How long did that owl circle hunting in search? He did not grow frustrated and quit. That wasn't an option. Keep searching. Keep holding the vision. That which I seek, is also seeking me.

July 3:

A heavy summer rain falls outside. I am grateful for the light captured in the round base of raindrops as they cling to the window pane. The sound of rain slapping onto broad maple leaves outside. The heady smell of parched forest quickly absorbing the generous rainfall. Summer sensory delights and the beauty of senses that can savour it.

Everything around me is alive... thriving... and unfolding.

<u>July 4:</u>   **NEW MOON**

★ NEW LUNAR CYCLE. NEW ENERGIES. NEW INTENTIONS:

- WHAT EMOTIONS DO I WANT TO EXPERIENCE IN THIS NEW CYCLE?
- WHAT CHANGES DO I WANT TO MAKE?
- WHAT DO I WANT TO ATTRACT? TO BUILD? TO CREATE? TO GROW?

Like my garden out back, I want to burst into vibrant bloom. I want to feel open to allowing beauty. To feel happy and abundant. *I want to feel joyous!*

Okay. I want to feel joyous. I want to feel good. How do I have the power to contribute to those sensations?

I can avoid situations that bring me down and lower my mood.

I can deliberately create situations and circumstance that will put me in a happier mindset.

I can pick my battles. I can opt out of most of them altogether.

I can make smarter choices. I *will* make smarter choices. I AM making smarter choices.

I can... I will.... I *am* embarking on this scavenger hunt with the Universe. Whatever makes me feel good or brings me joy, these are my clues. Exploring with great curiosity, following as though I am being pulled magnetically.

Earlier this week I realized I'd overlooked planting nasturtiums. One of my favourite plants. Today I was both delighted and surprised to discover the mysterious presence of nasturtium leaves hiding amidst my rows of rosemary plants. The large broad leaves of nasturtiums have always reminded me of smiling cartoon frog faces. I am captivated by how they hold water droplets. I am grateful for blooming daisies, gladioli greens stretching skyward adorned with tightly clenched buds, zucchini blossoms, and the unexpected discovery of nasturtiums.

July 5:

I envision a soft shield much like a blanket around my field of personal Energy. It is a soft and open weave and it is my filter from the Energies around me. It allows Love to freely pass through, able to receive and exchange with those around me. But this exquisitely fuzzy shield prevents angstful Energy from reaching me.

Breathing deeply, I give thanks for the various skills and visualizations in my repertoire. Giving thanks to floating atop of drama. Remaining buoyant and refusing to be pulled down into any of it. Sending blessings and Love Bubbles to all the amazing Souls throughout my Life who have instilled such powerful lessons.

I send Love and compassion out through my blanket's weave to the co-tenant.

I am grateful for peace.

July 6:

When I asked My Little Roommate today what she is grateful for she replied, "That home is coming our way!" Holding the vision with you Girl Child, holding the vision.

July 7:

I am grateful for the privilege of feeding My Little Roommates a deliciously home prepared meal. I am grateful all our needs are met and I am able to share the abundance with those around me regardless of any tension.

July 8:

I am grateful I can feel a noticeable shift in my mental Energies. The sweet relief that accompanies it is very much appreciated. I am grateful for the epiphany that my emotional state and my mental state are different entities. I am an embodiment of physical, spiritual, emotional and mental planes. I am grateful to be learning and unfolding.

July 9:

I am grateful that dog and I were not run over by an ATV charging along the winding forest access road. He didn't see us until I started waving my arms. We are safe and intact. We are happy. We are well hiked.

July 10:

Thunder has been clapping loudly and lightning illuminating the night sky tonight. My Little Roommate, with dog following close behind, joined us in the Magick Attick seeking familiar comfort. Four walls, a roof, windows, and an embrace to keep my babes and me safe and dry. I am loved. I am their safe harbour of refuge. I am humbled. I am so very deeply grateful.

July 11:

It was an unusual and rather spectacular treat today, with the co-tenant out and off the property for the entire day. No one but us! Pajama clad, snuggled, in our attic apartment. We haven't felt this free in months!

"Long may it be, the power of three!!! Grateful, grateful, grateful."

July 12:

Last month a family lost their dog Cara while vacationing here. They extended their stay for as long as they could, but there came a time that they sadly had to return home without her. A Facebook group "Bring Cara Home" has been created and nearly a thousand community members have joined, many keeping a watchful eye out for the dog.

Perhaps it is because of how displaced I feel from my own sense of home but I want nothing more than to see this dog reunited with her people. Her family has notified the public that she is skittish of other dogs and men, and they feel the best chance of Cara being found is by a lone woman... with snacks. Her last sighting is relatively nearby. So today I ventured out on my own without dog. Just me, my walking stick Gandalf, and a plastic bag of deli sandwich meats.

I head up Pell Road in Roberts Creek, and at the lower end there are other hikers and dogs out and about. I opt to drive up to the far end of the road in an effort to expand the search. In hindsight I should've opted to look on a day *other* than garbage day.

Walking down a dusty gravel road lined with thick forest. I am softly calling Cara's name aloud as I crinkle the bag of sandwich meats. I can't shake the sense that I am being watched but I can't see any eyes on me. Finally, something rustles in the bush, and I hear an audible "gruff" I'm so excited by the possibility that I've encountered this missing dog, it doesn't occur to me it could be anything *but* her. That is, until a black bear cub comes scrambling out of the bush and up a nearby tree, soon to be followed by another cub. Followed by a *third* scrambling cub.

I am filled with dread knowing that Mama Bear is near, but in this moment every instruction I ever received about what to do in the event of a bear encounter evaporates from my terrified mind. Without thinking, I throw my paltry bag of sandwich meat as my sacrificial offering in an unspoken exchange for my personal safety. Waving my walking stick about, trying not to panic and run. I walk as quickly as I can to cover the expansive distance of the dusty gravel road between myself, and my parked car.

Sorry Cara- I wish you well, but I'm out!

I am grateful to return home from my adventure unscathed. Though I am in no rush to head out into the forest without my dog again anytime soon. I am also especially grateful both my bladder and bowels co-operated maintaining their composure. I am grateful for whatever self dignity wasn't left on the trail. Next to that bag of sandwich meats.

<u>July 13</u>:

I remind myself this is merely a time of transition. I consider it a skill practice or practicum for all my life lessons thus far. Universal Law of Duality: there is Light, there is shadow, and that polarity will forever be a part of the human experience. I reassure myself that when we **do** meet home, we will have greater appreciation from this perspective broadening situation.

One of My Little Roommates announces fretfully, "We can't move before my friends come to camp out over the weekend". I have a similar response at the thought of leaving my blooming garden prematurely. I breathe. I trust. I cha cha cha.

Speaking with a friend today, from out of nowhere I am inclined to ask her if she has ever used a wood burning tool to draw on wooden spoons, and we chatted briefly about the possibilities. While the idea wasn't inspiring for her, I have not been able to shake the inspiration. I bought a wood burning tool today, and I am excited to explore this idea and indulge my need to create. I am grateful for sparks of inspiration that swirl within the imagination.

What a journey this is. We are so very blessed, even when we have to squint, tilt our heads to the left and refocus our soulful kaleidoscopes to be able to recognize it.

The blessings are *always* there.

July 14:

I claimed the time and the space for art making in the Magick Attick this afternoon. With a wooden spoon reclaimed from my kitchen drawer and my new pyrography tool. I emblazoned the Goddess symbol on the bowl of the spoon, and something whispered *"Spirit Spoon"* as I worked on it. I am inexplicably tickled with delight at the prospects.

Time in my garden sanctuary today found my sage, rosemary and lavender lush and thriving. I am looking forward to harvesting the herbs and bundling them when the time comes. As much as I want to move the thought of having to walk away from this garden saddens me.

Hey! I am back at that "half in-half out" place. I cannot co-create if I am not 100% committed to the vision. I am piecing together this puzzle of manifestation. I am excited by all of the unfolding possibilities and potential.

July 15:

In the midst of an emotionally strained moment, I was reminded to ask to see *the truth, the purity and the sincerity of this situation.* I am learning. May this somehow benefit the Highest Good of All involved. May I continue twisting and turning my soulful kaleidoscope until I am able to capture the gratitude and the Light seeping through the shards of a defaulted mindset. I remind myself I **choose** my perspective. I am deeply grateful for the reminder.

July 16:

My Little Roommates and I indulged in an act of curiosity this afternoon, pouring all the "grateful" squares onto my bed, sifting, sorting and counting. Even without opening any of them, I

bask in the knowing that each folded square contains an appreciation of a different blessing experienced within this strange year of
redirection.

July 17:

I am grateful to be exploring ways of balancing the varying needs
of My Little Roommates. I know the reality is siblings always feel
as though the other kid is the favourite. I accept this, though
I still hold the desire to find a harmonious peaceful midpoint.
It is like an antique weight scale: my needs and well being are
what the two platforms of their wellness needs hang from. If I
am going to try to meet their needs. It is crucial I meet my own
first. I am stepping into responsibility for that: my wellness must
be my first priority.

July 18:

It has been wonderful watching community rally to support this family's quest to reunite with their lost dog. I am grateful to read the family
is visiting the coast again this weekend. Camping in a borrowed trailer
in the area Cara was last seen. I have begun a little anticipatory wager
with myself: who will be reunited with home first, us or Cara? May
there be a happy ending for all.

July 19:   FULL BUCK MOON

★ FULL MOON REFLECTIONS:

○ HAVE MY EMOTIONAL EXPERIENCES BEEN WHAT I SET FORTH AS MY NEW MOON
  INTENTION?

○ HOW WILL I INFLUENCE MY EMOTIONAL EXPERIENCE?

○ HOW WILL I INITIATE MORE SELF-CARE?

○ WHAT WILL I DELEGATE, ASK FOR ASSISTANCE OR EVEN RELEASE?

The seeds I planted in May, I never dug them up to ensure they were growing. I never insisted on evidence to prove the garden was coming to fruition. I trusted, and today my garden is in full bloom. Am I releasing expectation? Am I holding true to trust? How can I support myself in this strange and mysterious unfolding?

I am grateful for the wide range of opportunities to be able to give back to my community: whether a $2 donation to the food bank, or a local busker, picking up litter along the side of the road, keeping a watchful eye out for a lost pet, or someone requiring assistance. Maybe it isn't the big things that will change the world, perhaps a series of small gestures around the globe. It starts here, with me, and this.

July 20:

My Little Roommates and I head down to the Roberts Creek mandala to participate in the community art project. I am wearing a Jimi Hendrix shirt I recently found in a thrift store. A guy approaches me to make small talk and inquire if I ever saw Hendrix perform live. I didn't say it aloud, but thought: He died in 1970, and I was born in 1973. I try not to be affected by his miscalculations. Opting instead to be complimented that he clearly thinks I look very well preserved. Perhaps I will save the t-shirt for yard work from now on.

Later in the day, driving down Beach Avenue, Roberts Creek with one of My Little Roommates, softly calling again for home.

"Home..... Hooommmmmeeeee".

We silence our calls as our car approaches a man walking alone. As we drive past he bellows loudly "it's coming!"

Turning and looking at one another, absolutely astonished, excitement tangible in the air. "Did you HEAR THAT?!?"

Synchronicities and flukes. At this point, I am not willing to discount or disregard anything we can derive hope from. Home is coming. Home is coming!!

We take the opportunity to hold thankful hearts for all the amazing things that are coming our way, that we as of today, don't have a single clue about.

July 21:

A woman tries to clamour over large beached logs scattered across Roberts Creek beach. She hollers, "Do I look responsible?!? I've got a beer and a child's bucket in the same hand!" Oh she made me *laugh!* Couldn't help but wonder what *would* be dropped first.

July 22:

I am grateful for the perfect beached log to stretch out on. Allowing my weary body a catnap after an early morning shift while My Little Roommate scampers across the beach. Winged insects flutter overhead pollinating as I drift off into a light sleep. My Little Roommate returns bearing a gift for me: an incredibly long and pristine white feather close to twelve inches long. We bring it back with us to the car placing it on the dashboard where a makeshift beach shrine has begun. A twisty piece of curly willow driftwood, joined by a rose bud I found one day severed from its shrub. Now this gift of a feather. It seems wherever we go an altar of one sort or another is created.

I am my own makeshift altar of gratitude.

July 23:

I am most joyous while floating in the starfish position, riding atop soft rolling waves, my hair fanned out about my face, the taste of ocean brine lingering on my lips. I manifest the most effectively, as in, the most quickly, when every cell of my Spirit and Being are vibrating in sheer and utter joy.

We have been domesticated. Brainwashed into complacency and frankly, there isn't enough joy in Life.

Play, dance, laugh, paint, love, do *something* today to create a pocket of bliss. Mid-euphoria, make a wish, release it and let it float off into the ether.

Then follow up that wish bubble you released into the world, with some small simple practical step that will bring you one step closer to the desired circumstance. Be mindful of the thoughts you are holding. If it is shaming, judgement or critical of yourself or others in *any* degree- drop it. Drop it fast. Drop it hard. Drop it with detachment, with compassion, with forgiveness. By that I mean, no follow up thoughts of "Oh I am such a _____ for thinking that" or some version thereof. Have compassion for yourself as you learn new ways of thinking. You wouldn't berate a small child learning how to walk. Embrace how adorable you are as you awkwardly learn new ways! Love yourself!

Create joy. Make a wish. Set it free. Follow it up with a simple step. Hold hopeful thoughts. Trust all is exactly as it should be in this very moment in your reality, for all to unfold for the Highest Good of All involved.

The Universal Law of Mental Gender decrees two things. First, whatever we plant will grow. You won't grow carrots planting turnip seeds. Second each unique creation has its own gestation period. Manifestation will take as long as it's going to take, but it will come to be. One way or the other. The question is, can I practice patience when I don't know the gestation period of what I am bringing forth?

I went through my stages of grieving and accepting this situation. I was sad. I was mad. I jumped on the blame train. Then I finally moved into acceptance. Throwing a temper tantrum isn't going to invoke change any faster, and so I harness all of my Energies, both internally and externally, to navigate, co-create, and invoke change. I am trying to do it playfully, and with a sense of wonder, nearly like a game of ping pong with the Universe. I put out to it exactly what I yearn for, it responds with a sign, I bounce back the strengthened intention accompanied by my offerings of gratitude. It bounces back another alternative.

That which I seek, is also seeking me, and I am so stoked for the day we connect. For it is already mine, I just haven't met it yet.

July 24:

A day of play the three of us, and dog, frolicking and rolling in the soft surging surf of a low tide. My Little Roommate exclaims jubilantly, "Mom's going in?!?! I LOVE IT when Mom goes in!" Sparks of joy and jubilation shoot off of our beings into the ether. I give deep thanks, deep love. Deep awe.

July 25:

Some drive cars. Some fly planes. Some sail boats. Navigation is necessary. Maps. Tools. Direction. Where are we now? Where do we want to go? What route am I embarking on? Do I want to find a shortcut, or do I want to explore the scenic route?

I am grateful for the appreciation that my emotions are the compass to my map. I am grateful for the knowing that my choices are my method of transportation. I am grateful for the insight that the people I surround myself with, either help to fill up my gas tank or deplete it.

Am I being honest with myself as to where I really want to go?

Am I making proactive empowered choices?

Am I recognizing that I am not my thoughts?

Better yet: am I selectively choosing the thoughts that I hold and releasing those that bring me grief?

I am grateful to be brave enough to hold myself accountable. I am grateful for the adventure of deliberate creation. This Life is my greatest work of art. My greatest adventure.

I will chart it carefully.

I breathe and trust and will celebrate with great gratitude.

Life isn't just happenstance. I got us into this with my good intentions, and now, it is up to sail and harness powerful winds of change. To very carefully chart the direction I wish to pursue. The time has come for me to work towards my own dream, not be employed to help achieve someone elses. It is time I heed my Soul's calling.

I want to utilize the skills I developed while earning my life coaching diploma. I want to inspire mindfulness and gratitude, and share the philosophy of Universal Law. I want to be creative and sell my magickal wares at local craft fairs.

I have no idea what that specifically looks like.

But I will know what it will FEEL like. If I can generate that emotional experience as often as I can, then I am more likely to bring the dreams to fruition.

I am grateful for the opportunity to work with a life strategist. Grateful for the planning, strategizing, scheduling and taking perfectly imperfect action.

The Life of my dreams is pulling me, and I will heed the pull. I am heeding the pull!

I have come to accept that I need to broaden my search for home. My early morning absences are fine now but when My Little Room-mates return to school in September it will complicate things. While it seems most counter intuitive, I am going to resign from my employment. Not many people understand my choice. I am mindful not to buy into their opinions or concerns, instead, I try to hold the faith that I can trust my own inner guidance. I am considering declaring myself a sovereign *no opinion zone*. I breathe. I trust. I cha cha cha.

July 26:

As I countdown the last of my early morning shifts, My Little Room-mate counts down until her friends campout on the acreage for the weekend. Anticipation, excitement and adventure hang in the air.

As of today, I have Spirit Spoons in six different test kitchens. Putting them through a rigorous domestic practicum to ensure the pyro-graphed images do not fade and that I can promote these as fully functional kitchen utensils. I am grateful for helpful volunteers!

July 27:

I awoke all flustered and goose pimply after a night of hot and heavy dreams. I miss sensual desire. I miss romance and intimacy, sharing physical passion and sexual climax. I am grateful for wet sweaty dreams. Thank Goddess for small blissful favours. One day again. One day.

July 28:

Someone in the community, not even an acquaintance, said something utterly daft and absurd to me. I am grateful I let the negative comment bounce right off of me. I imagine insensitive opinions flapping like flags in the wind. I can't stop the wind. Flags are gonna flap. Ain't no sense in being affected or offended by it. One of My Little Roommates even commented about it hours later over dinner. I am being watched, and they are observing and learning. I am grateful.

July 29:

I am grateful for the symphonic sounds of life: the wind rustling through the leaves outside the window of the Magick Attick, the sleepy grunts of a Little Roommate gently stretching as she softly awakens to this new day.

While I am surrounded by sweet simple sounds there seems to be a no-holds barred game of dodgeball going on within the dualities of my psyche. Light versus the shadow. It seems as though the "dark side" has more muscle power. But this is just a piece of the complex illusion. I remind myself *whichever* side I focus on is the one with the secret superpower. So I harness my focus wisely. Sending extra moxie to my internal Light Workers. It can't be easy being the warm and fuzzy feelings up there so I infuse them with Love, stardust, encouragement and good wishes. We *got* this. Anything different is an illusion that I will not support with my Energy or attention.

This Life, this transition is going to be just as easy as I tell myself it is or just as difficult as I tell myself it shall be. In that choice therein lies my power. I give thanks for this insight.

July 30:

I am a rehabilitating city slicker privileged to know only the very top of the food chain. For the last eighteen days I have been contending with psychological post bear encounter trauma. Having unintentionally snuck up on a family of them sending her cubs scrambling up a tree in response to my appearance on the trail.

It was a breathtaking experience. Not the romantic kind.

I haven't been back into the forest since, which is unfortunate, my time there is a big investment in my well being. It is my church. My sacred chapel. My worship. My reverence. Soul food. I tried to visit again a few days ago but anxiety got the better of me. I turned back with dog and a heavy sense of compassion for myself.

Yesterday a bell bracelet similar to something you'd find in a kindergarten concert found me at a thrift store. I enthusiastically brought it home with me in the hopes of never sneaking up on a bear again.

Today I made as much racket along the narrow trail as a 1970's Hare Krishna jingling in an airport. I sang. I sang loudly, I sang badly, I sang proudly. Needless to say the only thing beyond canine company this morning was the briefest accompaniment of chickadees. I tried to enjoy them, but all I could remember was robins chirping loudly during my bear encounter.

You should have seen me jump when branches snapped in the distance. I picked up my pace, tightened the waistband of my big girl pants, and forced myself to continue. I tried to distract myself with a scavenger hunt of mushrooms, heart shaped rocks and shelf fungi.

Self-prescribed forest immersion therapy was the only way I was going to be able to move through this. I cough. I talk aloud. I sweat, leaving an aromatic wake of wild woman body odour behind me. We make it to our sweet spot along the edge of the creek. Dog happily slurps the cool fresh running water, and I sip it from cupped hands. The smell of dense forest embraces us amid the summer humidity.

Turning back I walk through the depths of green again before making our way back to the mouth of the forest. Slowly, up hill, the jingle of my wrist, the tap of my walking stick, the crunch of my step, a pep talk crossing my lips aloud. Again, not surprisingly, no animal encounter.

We are back on the broad dirt trail and I finally relax a bit knowing that I have greater odds of encountering a weekend warrior on an all terrain vehicle or dirt bike. On my way out I collect a fallen piece of wood that has been calling to me for weeks. I carry this slab of lumber tucked beneath my arm adorned with bells. For the first time this hike, it is just the sounds of my breath, dog panting, the tap of my staff and the crunch of my steps. We continue on silently, the prickle of the wood's cut edge rubbing against my inner arm. I am trying not to be disappointed there was no message bestowed on me this time. Although what could one expect with my clamour?

We reach the mouth of the bush exiting onto the forest access road. A white tailed deer saunters down the middle of the road. She doesn't have the opportunity to see me or my leashed dog before a pickup truck barrels around the bend of the gravel road, screeching to a halt to avoid hitting her. Dust rises in a thick cloud. She stands there, stunned like the proverbial deer in headlights. Under normal circumstances, she would have run away from us. But after a split nanosecond heavy with suspense, the deer bolts bounding straight towards us less than an arm's length away. Dog goes nuts with alarm, excitement and intrigue. The startled deer leaps effortlessly. Disappearing with camouflaged ease and grace. The only evidence remains is the swaying bush and the rippled air from her streaking past us.

"*Oh Dear*" Intuition whispers to me, "*You passed through fear and found magick on the other side*".

Oh deer, indeed.

August
2016

"SHE GROWS"

August 1:

For the last couple of months I have been working on a written piece called "She Grows". It is my heartfelt memoir of excavating to clear the garden and what I ended up unearthing within myself. Winged ones buzzed and hovered from blossom to blossom this afternoon as I sat in the lush garden completing one of the black and white line drawings for the booklet. I am grateful for the inspiration my garden provides me. Grateful it whispers encouragement and soulful messages to me as much as the forest does.

August 2:   NEW MOON

★ NEW MOON. NEW ENERGIES. NEW INTENTIONS:

- IN THIS NEW UNFOLDING CYCLE, WHAT IS MY DESIRED EXPERIENCE?
- WHAT EMOTIONAL EXPERIENCES AM I YEARNING FOR?
- WHAT AM I LOOKING TO ACHIEVE AND ACCOMPLISH?
- WHAT ACTIONS DO I NEED TO TAKE TO DO SO?
- WHAT SCENARIOS CAN I CREATE TO POSITIVELY INFLUENCE MY EMOTIONAL EXPERIENCE?

I am grateful for a cacophony of duck quacks riding the wind over treetops this afternoon.

A couple of weeks back a friend told me about a ritual for attracting money. Back in the day of dollar bills, circles would shower each member one at a time with paper currency. The sensation of money raining down increasing the magnetic pull attracting such. The other day, I cashed my paycheck in five dollar bills. The facial expression on the bank teller was priceless! Tonight My Little Roommates and I all took turns having the experience of being showered by one hundred and twenty $5 bills, as we all exuberantly declared "we attract and receive so easily and abundantly!" We laughed. We squealed. We writhed in puddles of money.

I am so grateful I have the freedom to raise them in an open minded manner. I am also grateful for the sensation of money raining down on me.

August 3:

I am grateful for time to work on the unfolding development of "She Grows". Brainstorming pages of mind dump describing wrestling to remove the blackberry thicket. I am struggling with advancing, but tonight in my gratefuls, instead of focusing on the confusion, I write *"I look forward to resolution...."*

August 4:

I have blossomed into a woman beyond anything I ever dared to imagine or dream. I am grateful.

August 5:

I am shedding beliefs that no longer serve me. Don't look back wistfully at what I have outgrown and shed. Slither forward woman. Slither ever onward in gratitude.

August 6:

One of My Little Roommates declares tonight, "I love helping you with your gratefuls". Collaboration!

Thumpity thump thump
Thumpity thump thump
Beats my grateful, grateful heart.

August 7:

I have created a tear off calendar counting down the number of early morning shifts remaining. Each morning at 5am, I bumble and stumble down from the Magick Attick to my coffee maker in the basement Girl Cafe, where I ceremoniously tear off another square. As of today, only ten shifts remain! I am so, so exhausted. But this too shall pass and new adventures await!

August 8:

Still not knowing where we will be moving to I rented a post office box for a year today. At least the mail will have somewhere to call home. I joke about holding a house warming party for the post office box. Maybe put a tiny Persian rug on the floor of the narrow metal box. I am grateful for the relief laughter can bring during awkward strained periods.

August 9:

When dramatic stuff swirls about, I am grateful for the insight to remind myself, *"I am not in this!"*. I am grateful for the realization it is happening *around* me. I am not in it. Thereby refusing to allow my emotional state to be impacted by it.

August 10:

A rough draft of a tag for Spirit Spoons was drafted today. I am excited by this endeavour!

August 11:

An astrologer reminds me in his latest video, *"Are you going to take the train back to your past, or are you going to take the train into your future?!?"* I don't want to go backwards. I am grateful for the reminder.

Onward!!!

August 12:

My Little Roommates and I camped out last night to watch a meteor shower. We created a warm nest of pillows, blankets and sleeping bags on the trampoline. Curled up together beneath a sky of shooting stars. Easily sharing daydreams and wishes before we gradually drifted to sleep one by one.

This morning I awoke to daybreak unfolding. A precious Girl Child on either side of me. I lay there lazily relishing the moment. No matter how old your babies are, it's always blissful watching them sleep. A big grin spreads across one of their faces and she starts to laugh heartily in her sleep. Behold: a moment even more pure than watching a puppy dream animatedly!

I wish I could bottle the essence of this moment. So when the depths of Winter are upon us, I can uncork it and sniff the enchantment of the moment again.

August 13:

"Are you done?" a vexed Little Roommate barks frustrated at me mid-argument. "You tell me not to be clenched and uptight! I manage to unclench for a moment, only for you to say something that clenches me up again!!"

Whoa Nelly. An Ocean of Estrogen indeed. We are both learning to navigate the uncertain terrain of a mother daughter relationship within the mountainous territory of teenage years. I am grateful for communication and cooperative navigation.

Adventure is in the air!

August 14:

A day trip to visit our favourite swimming lake again. When we are there we are so happy it feels as though our Souls are shooting off fireworks. Emotional sparks of pure joy and elation soaring through the summer sky. I am grateful my girls are strong enough swimmers that I can leave them together unattended and I venture further out to swim alone. As soon as I am away from the shore I slip out of my bathing suit, loop it over my arm, and glide through the beautiful lake skyclad and unencumbered.

When I swim alone I transport myself back to carefree days. Any troubles, worries and responsibilities dissolve in my wake. On my return approach the beams of late afternoon sunshine cascade around my body. Cutting through the depths below like a heavenly aura around my splayed breast stroking silhouette. Dragonflies hover overhead like a crown. I am so freaking crazy grateful for this majestic lake. It is some powerful medicine indeed.

August 15:

I am grateful I am learning to embrace compassion over judgement. Sometimes you can't make stuff happen. It isn't black and white. I am grateful for the lesson. Is this why home has not yet appeared? I am learning, but I wonder if perhaps it is not just my lesson to be learnt. Perhaps I am facilitating another's life lesson. I cling to trust, hope, and optimism. I have begun collecting as many cardboard boxes as I can, I want to pack as much as possible, so that when "home" appears, *and it will*, we can pounce on it. I am grateful.

August 16:

I am beyond frustrated and stretched in this living situation. With zero tolerance *this* is the danger time of me doing something impulsive. I am grateful for mindfulness and self-awareness. I will breathe. I will float. What I think: I create. I know this too shall pass. I can feel it in the marrow of my wild woman bones.

I practice patience. I breathe fully and deeply. The kind of inhalations that graze my rib cage; my expanding lungs bumping into the arches of my feet from the inside. The kind of deep exhalations that send leaves scurrying from tree branches and send clouds swooshing across blue skies. I practice patience.

<u>August 17:</u>

I dreamt of moving last night. Dreamt of a freshly painted tall white walls in a small vibrant space. High ceilings and lots of Light. Daylight was flooding into the space. In the dream, we had just moved all of our boxes in, and I was excited to be showing the space to a friend. I laughed upon waking because we *must* have been in the process of moving in the dream. There is no way I would have company over with everything still in stacks of cardboard boxes.

The moment I opened my eyes, my day immediately started with happy gratitude.

One day closer.

"That which I seek, is also seeking me"

<u>August 18:</u>   **FULL STURGEON MOON**

★ FULL MOON REFLECTIONS:

- ○ HAVE I BEEN EXPERIENCING THE EMOTIONS I DECLARED AS MY NEW MOON INTENTIONS?
- ○ AM I MINDFULLY USING MY POWERS FOR GOOD?
- ○ AM I USING MY TIME WISELY?
- ○ WHAT DISTRACTIONS HAVE I LOADED ONTO MY PLATE?
- ○ IS MY PLATE FULL OF WHAT I LOVE AND WILL SAVOUR? OR AM I MAKING MYSELF EAT SOMETHING I DON'T LIKE?
- ○ WHAT DO I GIVE MYSELF PERMISSION TO CLEAR OFF INTO THE COMPOST?

Friends of My Little Roommate are camping in the yard for the next two nights. Alright Universe, that was the deal. She got her campout. Now we find home.

We had the quintessential summer day at the beach. The sun was shining without a cloud in the sky, the smell of seaweed and saltwater hung thick in the air and the tide was as far out as I had ever seen it. Walking out to the water's edge, we waded out until we could submerge ourselves. Swimming out to the horizon where we were being observed by a particularly curious and playful sea otter. I am grateful for safe distances between wildlife and myself.

After our extensive swim we returned to the shore where the girls scurried and frolicked around sandbars cluttered with large purple starfish. Lifting seaweed coated, barnacle encrusted rocks exploring the microcosm of scurrying marine life beneath. I took the opportunity to sit cross-legged amongst a cove of large rocks, meditating as the tide slowly came up around my waist, happy to be anchored within the four elements: the fiery Sun, the salt Water, the sandy Earth beneath me, and the deep inhalation and exhalation of ocean Air. By the time we were done, I had a suntan line of my necklace pendant on my chest. It was an amazingly beautiful peaceful family day and I overflow with gratitude.

August 19:

Tonight I sit in bed perched against stacked cushions writing my gratefuls by the soft glow of a bedside lamp. The slanted ceiling overhead covered with a fluttering swarm of moths batting against a hung tapestry. One of My Little Roommates comes over to ask me something and is in awe of all the fluttering wings overhead.

"Wow! There aren't any over on my side of the room. They must *really* like you!!"

I am preparing for my own metamorphosis. I am grateful for their wing flapping reminders.

August 20:

We are hanging out together in our downstairs Girls Café. Normally I wouldn't intentionally spend a magnificent summer evening here. But we await the live broadcast of the Tragically Hip's final concert. We have often daydreamed the three of us, chattering about which musical acts we would want to see in concert as a family. The Tragically Hip has always been one of my first choices. Their music has been a staple to the soundtrack of my children's lives.

The announcement of lead singer Gord Downie's diagnosis of terminal brain cancer has the country reeling at this vibrant talent's plight in his prime. Concert tickets were immediately snagged by scalpers to the disappointment of many fans. The country was further moved by the band's generosity of Spirit; broadcasting their final show sharing it with us in our homes.

Dinner simmers on the hotplate as the one I have affectionately called "Lil Bones" all her life, swirls, and dances with me atop our area rug to the performance of "Lil Bones." My eyes well. I had always hoped to share a dance with her to a live performance of this song. This isn't remotely how I imagined it, but so it goes with life: often not quite how we anticipated it.

I press this memory, this dance, this song, this freeze frame moment of time with her. With them. The three of us. Pressing it deeply into my heart. Tucked betwixt and between layers of tissue, like how one would press a flower between book pages. I will cherish this memory, for the rest of my days.

August 21:

I rearranged the furniture in the Magick Attick last night. When we had the cabin to ourselves we pushed furniture and broadened the goat trails between towers of cardboard boxes so we could we lug a large chesterfield and a plush love seat down two steep flights of stairs into the basement. The Little Roommate that had been residing in the basement has joined us in the Magick Attick. I am thrilled to bits she is joining us in our upstairs nest and at the same time I am grateful that the large and cumbersome couches will be that much easier to vacate from the space when "home" appears.

I am grateful I slept the whole night through and didn't wake up and crash into anything in a half asleep bumbling state trying to make my way down the stairs to the bathroom.

August 22:

I am learning to experience feelings without judging them. They come to me, with me, and away from me. This too shall pass. I practice compassion for myself. I am grateful for emotional awareness.

August 23:

Back at our favourite lake again today deliberately creating joyful emotional states: the sound of the lake lapping on the rock, the good fortune of immersing myself and My Little Roommates in those pristine waters again.

August 24:

Before heading into work for 6am I take ten minutes at the beach. I walk the length of the pier, savour the 5:30am early morning sunrise, fill my lungs with fresh ocean air and ground myself in my footsteps. Returning from my walk I am approached by a sleepy eyed pajama clad beautiful hippie swaddled in a blanket. She asks me if I'd like to join her on a log beneath her blanket and watch the sunrise unfold. Alas, I did the responsible thing. Explained I was on my way to work, and carried on my way. I am flattered by her invitation and I hope she has a beautiful day.

Classifieds advertising rental housing are slowly beginning to appear. I can't help but do a hopeful happy dance behind the hotel front desk to the delight of my coworkers and supervisor.

That which I seek is also seeking me.

August 25:

We visited a friend's thrift store today. As we left a gust of wind sailed through the open car windows blowing the large white feather off the dashboard, out the window and into the parking lot. My heart wilted for a moment at the loss, but I remind myself a profound lesson I am learning this year: attachment to things is a slippery slope. I give thanks for the expression of Love that resulted in the feather being gifted to me and the time I shared with it. Thank you feather for hanging out with us as long as you did. I hope you enjoy your adventures. I choose to hold a grateful mind, heart and Spirit.

August 26:

Before heading home from work, I stop at a neighbourhood beach for a moment of solitude. Breathing deep, silencing a racing mind before transitioning from the shifts of employee to that of motherhood. I am grateful to pause and mark the transition. To feel the wind blowing upon my skin. The sound of crashing surf fills my ears and sunlight glows softly through my closed eyelids. I polish my armour before returning to the cardboard chaos of the collector's cabin.

I embraced adventure today! Commemorated the last day of my 42nd year by having my nose pierced. This definitely seemed the type of year to acknowledge by paying someone to punch a hole through my nostril.

August 27:

We celebrated my 43rd birthday at our favourite lake today. Any day spent there is a good day indeed. We had dinner from our favourite burger truck at a picnic table in a small village square accompanied by chocolate birthday cake from the bakery of the grocery store across the way. I am grateful for this beautiful birthday with my loves. I wouldn't have wished for it any other way.

August 28:

The three of us hanging out in the Magick Attick and I consider aloud, "Maybe we haven't found home because we are looking in the wrong spot?" I immediately have their undivided attention their intrigue evident through raised eyebrows.

"If you could live anywhere on the coast, what school would you each be happiest in?".

One replies faster than the other, but it is unanimous; they want to return to their old schools. And so it is decided, the geographic search for home will be broadened, expanded and refocused. I commit, right then and there, to registering them in the schools of their choice and doing the long distance commute to get them there daily.

"This is how it will manifest," I tell a friend confidently. "This is how the Universe will know I mean business."

I revise the desired location on my *"Have You Seen Our Home?"* poster and begin plastering it in our new target area.

No judgements. Simple compassion for all involved. Evidently we are just standing in the wrong aisle of the manifestation grocery store. I remind myself: everything changes. Even when we don't want it to. I hold dear to the faith that "home" is coming then I scramble to register them for their schools of preference less than a week before school returns to session.

That which I seek is also seeking me....

<u>August 29:</u>

I am grateful to have shared a meal today, that My Little Roommates dubbed "DUNCH".

If brunch is a late breakfast combined with an early lunch, then "dunch" is a late lunch combined with an early dinner. We dined and saw the seasonal spectacle of a turquoise ocean. It was an exquisite sight. Visiting our friend's thrift store again, I'm suddenly and mysteriously inclined to ask if my large white feather has been seen. Explaining that it blew out my car window at the end of our last visit.

"That is so wild you ask!" her face lights up animatedly, "I have seen it tumbling around the shop floor for the last few days. Right before you pulled in and parked, it caught an air stream from the front and back doors perched open, and swirled up, up and around in the air. Here you are asking for it. That's some wild magick! Unlike *anything* I've ever seen!"

I am grateful to have been reunited with the beautiful feather and I am grateful to have bestowed a glimpse of my magick to another.

<u>August 30:</u>

I sit on the pier at early dawn this morning in an overwhelmed dither. My Little Roommates are back at the cabin sleeping soundly. I prefer to schedule my emotional breakdowns, moments when my cheese slips off of my cracker, away from their eyes as best I can. I know they are stressed. They don't need my emotions compounding their sadness. Softly speaking aloud, crying, I ask for a sign. I turn my head, and there is a cloud in the perfect formation of an angel's wing. It was so prominent I gasped aloud when I saw it. My conversations with a playful co-creating Universe continues. I hold optimism home is coming. I ask for strength to continue with grace and do no harm. I am beyond grateful for the hope that sign filled me with. I breathe... I trust..... I cha cha cha.

I got this I sniffle bravely to myself.

August 31:

Laying in bed in the dark a moth's wings are fluttering in flight just above my ear. The sound is accompanied by the slightest breeze from wings tickling my neck. The moth has me considering where I am in my own cycle of metamorphosis, I hope I am ready to burst free from the tight bind of my cocoon. I am grateful for my health and the symphony of my five senses.

I want to fly. I *will* fly. Soon. Change is inevitable.

I am grateful for the flow of rhythms and cycles. The knowledge that sooner or later everything comes to pass. Please, Mother Father Creator, All my Spirit Guides, please help me through this. I know it has to be for the Highest Good of All, even though I don't understand. All I can do is take radical responsibility towards my well being and that of my daughters, All I can do is breathe deeply, be good to myself, and keep on twisting and turning my soulful kalcidoscope as I wait for this to pass. The only way out is through.

September
2016

"SHUFFLING AND SORTING"

September 1:

★ NEW MOON. NEW CYCLES. NEW ENERGIES. NEW INTENTIONS:

- HOW DO I WANT TO FEEL THROUGHOUT THIS NEW LUNAR CYCLE?
- WHAT DO I WANT TO ACCOMPLISH?
- ARE MY ACTIONS CONGRUENT WITH THE ABOVE?

My biggest goal for this cycle is to create the inventory of Spirit Spoons needed for the craft fair the first week of November. Every spare moment I have, I am either hiking in the forest or pyrographing spoons. It is important to me that I still maintain my self-care while creating the necessary stock.

In our makeshift kitchen one stressed out Little Roommate declares sincerely to her sister "I am sorry I snapped at you. I haven't done this before. I should have tried better." Then she brings her sister back to the dinner table to make peace and break bread. My heart melted at the display, the accountability, the making peace. We are all learning new ways. I am grateful.

September 2:

Some days are tougher than others, when you want so desperately to make something happen and Life seems in a perpetual stall. I was sitting on the front porch. Taking a moment to myself to settle some big feelings.

"I really need a pep talk" I say aloud in my hurting state.

I go inside and upstairs to cuddle with a Little Roommate who is feeling under the weather. I offer her a cough drop, and when I unwrap it, it says on the inside of the wrapper *"A pep talk with every drop".*

Tears of frustration mixed with hope and gratitude cascade freely down my cheeks. Conversations with a playful co-creating Universe continue.

September 3:

Driving up the rough road towards our dirt driveway, a coyote steps out of the greenery and crosses the road just ahead of my vehicle. I am grateful for the mysterious encounter. Dear Universe: I am watching. I am listening. I am waiting. I am willing.

Thank you.

Thank you. Thank you. Thank you.

September 4:

Through the large window overlooking the backyard I watch a mother black bear accompanied by her two cubs scrambling over the fence and ambling into our yard. Very quietly I call my girls to join me in watching this amazing sight.

Mother Bear climbs a fruit tree, her cubs waiting below. Bouncing on the hunched tree trunk she knocks the fruit off onto the ground below. We wait, awestruck, wondering if the tree will snap beneath her girth. Before it does, she simply steps off the top of the tree which is touching the ground and joins her cubs in their picnic lunch.

"Just like us" one of My Little Roommates says, "A Mama and her two cubs".

Silently I wrap my arms around their shoulders, gently squeezing my cubs.

Love Bubbles to all.

September 5:

"Jessie's Girl" was playing on the car radio. I put in a CD. From the backseat one of My Little Roommates protests, "Hey! I was listening to that!"

We get into the grocery store. "Jessie's Girl" starts playing on the store speakers. She lets out a hushed little squeal and does a little dance. Well manifested Girl Child, well manifested!

September 6:

Today is the first day of our long distance commute to their "happy schools". Leaving at 7:15am to get my first Little Roommate to school for 8:15, then driving another forty minutes to get the other Little Roommate to her school for a 9am start.

I plan on spending the day on the road or in the forest. It makes no sense to return to the cabin only to turn around and do the epic journey again. Not that *any* of this makes sense at this point in time. I remind myself I am shuffling and sorting. Sometimes we have to identify what we *don't* want, to better identify what we DO want.

I am excited to reconnect with my favourite patch of forest. It seems I'd just recognized the soulful medicine I felt I received there before moving away. I have been working on forgiving myself, I hope she can forgive me too.

"I'm coming back forest! I'm coming!!"

My preparations for my day on the road include: lunch for myself, hiking clothes, something dry to change into after I hike up a sweat. A dog leash, bottled water for myself and dog, dog food, my tarot cards, the favourite of my smaller crystals, an audio book, my iPod, a sketchbook, my journal and an array of pens, pencils, erasers and other miscellaneous art supplies. By the time I am packed I look like I am embarking on a daytrip. But wait! I am!! My art studio on the go.

I give deep thanks that I have the ability to do this for my family. I am rebuilding a Life that indeed *will* reflect the Highest Good of All. I hold the vision with a grateful heart.

Thank you Mother Father Creator.
Thank you my 'Beloved I Am Presence'.
I hold deep reverence and gratitude.
The unfolding continues.

September 7:

Last Autumn I was asked to describe my ideal day. I remember describing morning hikes in the forest with dog, followed by afternoons of writing or making art. It dawns on me that as I wait on the far end of the coast for the end of their school days, I have unknowingly created very close to my ideal day. Hiking in the mornings followed by an afternoon of creativity in my car. I am learning the importance of being very specific when describing ideals. An art studio would be a far more comfortable workspace than inside my sedan. I am grateful for the Universe's playful sense of humour.

Note to self: *next time be really, REALLY specific.*

September 8:

Full circle moment. Picking up My Little Roommates from the YMCA Elphinstone camp this afternoon. I remember standing there five years earlier, having travelled to attend Diabetes Family Camp, wistfully declaring to myself *"I'd love to live here one day"*. Look what we did! I had no idea when I uttered that wish that I would years later reduce our household belongings by fifty percent so we could cram it all onto a BC Ferry and relocate to the Sunshine Coast. Grateful, grateful, grateful!! Now, to get out of this strange living situation and find HOME. I breathe and I trust and cha cha cha.

"That which I seek, is also seeking me."

September 9:

Oh Monkey Mind, we meet again.

I am grateful I can hear and see what it is trying to pull in my mind right now. I'm not buying into it. Bellowing sternly like an ancient queen to a member of her court I demand:

"What evidence do you have to support your claims?"

Alas, it has nothing to back up its fear. It scurries back into the shadows. I breathe. I release.

September 10:

"Cara is home! Cara is home!" one of My Little Roommates bellows across the Magick Attick.

Three months after the dog went missing, she turned up today in a Halfmoon Bay backyard, more than 25 kilometeres from where she went missing.

"I'm so happy that was the first thing on my FaceBook news feed!" she exclaims happily.

Grateful for happy reunions. Cara is home... our turn is coming.

September 11:

I am grateful I recognized an anxious mental worry moment in my head. Here we go again, *"Hey- Monkey Mind. What evidence do you have to support your claims?"*

Nothing is forthcoming. I go out to the backyard to watch my wishing ribbons billow over my garden in the wind.

I breathe... I trust... I cha cha cha.

September 12:

A mock up copy of my illustrated booklet "She Grows" was printed up today. I celebrate progress and momentum. I recognize the project has been a significant part of my coping. Coping that is necessary due to the home environment. Amazing gifts are presenting from this strange experience. I don't lose sight of that for a moment. I give deep, deep thanks.

September 13:

I inquired about the application process of a very popular craft fair, only to learn that today is the application deadline! Challenge accepted! I got it submitted in time, to quote a children's fairy tale: *just by the hair of my chinny-chin-chin.*

September 14:

I received word today I was accepted into the craft fair. Something in the marrow of my bones tells me that this is a key piece to my next chapter. I have no idea what that means, but I am excited to see who I will meet. That much I know to be true: it will be a "who".

Grateful, grateful, grateful.

September 15:

My Little Roommates hangs up the telephone and announces,

"DaddyMan is lost"

"I can relate" I reply.

She laughs, "No really, he's lost in the Simon Fraser University parking lot".

"Oh!" Laughter reverberates throughout the Magick Attick.

September 16:   **FULL HARVEST MOON**

★ FULL MOON REFLECTIONS:

- ○ HAVE I FELT THE WAY I SET AS MY INTENTION WITH THE NEW MOON?
- ○ HAVE MY ACTIONS CONTRIBUTED TO MY WILDEST DESIRES?
- ○ WHAT PROGRESS CAN I CELEBRATE AT THIS TIME?

After dark I made a point of setting time aside for me to go to the pier. To sit beneath the luminescent beauty of the Harvest Full Moon. Magick and splendour is afoot. I can feel it in my bones.

I bloom wherever I am planted.
I am my own favourite flowering bulb.
I am healthy.
I am majestic.
I am grateful.

September 18:

Today I sat in my garden picking herbs to wrap sage bundles.

We received our first ever response to the "Have You Seen Our Home?" poster. My Little Roommates and I sit perched together on the steep stairwell leading to the Magick Attick, reading the description of a prospective rental house. The description fits precisely what we are looking for.

I am grateful for possibility and for the aroma of freshly rolled bundles hanging to dry.

September 19:

I am, we are, grateful for the opportunity to view a rental house tomorrow. Please let this be it.

Please, please, please, please, *please*.....

September 20:

Last full day of Summer, tomorrow is the Autumn Equinox. I am grateful for all our seasonal adventures! Beautiful days immersed in exquisite bodies of water, and the many offerings of zucchini, green beans, lettuces and herbs from my garden.

September 21:   *AUTUMN EQUINOX*

I don't need to know where any of this is going right now. Breathe. Trust. I was reminded today of my manifestation ability. Reminded to do what I REALLY want. Hold the vision of where I want this to go, and take small tangible, perfectly imperfect flawed steps in that direction.

Why be content doing what I DON'T want to be doing?

I am grateful for the reminder.

September 22:

I am grateful every time I recognize the Inner Critic in my head commenting on my art, my writing, my Soul's expression, I announce, aloud, *"I am open to allowing and expressing my creativity!"* I imagine the Critic blinking in disbelief not certain how to reply to *that*.

September 23:

A teacher ran out to the parking lot when I dropped off My Little Roommate at school today.

"I wanted to introduce myself," he began "And I wanted to tell you...I have seen the results of a lot of different parenting styles. You have an amazing young lady, and I wanted to let you know, you are doing an awesome job."

I was speechless, and honestly, I welled up a bit. Motherhood has been the *toughest* thing I have ever done, certainly through the teenage years. I am grateful for his kind encouragement.

September 24:

I am grateful for how many people are holding the vision of us finding the perfect home for the Highest Good of All involved.

September 25:

Three times this week I have been told, "Thank you for sharing your artistic talents". Wow! Dear Inner Critic: How's **that** for validating evidence? I am grateful for reassurance and encouragement!

September 26:

Recently I've learned that when I am worried or fretting I am emitting a vibration of resistance. Today I caught myself in a moment of angst and opted to care for myself by going for a nap. When I awoke, there was a Spirit Spoon order from Colorado. I laughed at the timing of the lesson and the supporting evidence. I am grateful to be learning new ways. Grateful!!!

September 27:

I am waiting.

I am waiting in SO many areas of my life right now it is nearly comical. Nearly.

Waiting for a home.

Waiting for a mechanic to resolve a transmission issue.

"Trying to hit a moving target," was the exact quote. It has been three weeks.

Waiting for the next shipment of the utensils I use to make Spirit Spoons. I am told it will be at least another week.

Waiting for a telephone call regarding any or all of the above.

Time has been moving verrrrry slowwwwwwly.

There is nothing I can do to nudge any of it along, it's going to take however long it is going to take, and clearly, it's not going according to my agenda or timeline.

It reminds me of that point, when the bud is just about to burst open into bloom. But it's... just... not... quite... there.

So I influence what I can in this present moment. Instead of fretting about delays, I amp up my self-care. Listening extra carefully to what stories I am muttering in the back of my mind. When they are stories of limitation or lack, I consciously opt to lay them down.

Holding the vision of the bud gracefully blossoming with ease. As I practice patience, I scatter seeds in my fertile imagination as to what I want to grow next.

Is it easy? Absolutely not.

Is it worthwhile? It's certainly better than stressed clenching!

I am learning to shift my thoughts to allow expansion. I am not here in this Life, WE are not here in our Life, to worry or stress. WE are here to create, to express and to thrive.

I take a moment to give thanks for this Life lived thus far and for all the goodness that surely will follow.

I breathe. I trust. I cha cha cha.

September 28:

After four long days of waiting and wondering, I came home to a voicemail that the rental house was no longer available. We feel disappointed and defeated. Especially my daughters. Trapped. I feel like I could vomit... but at least there is no more wondering. We have clarity of sorts. This MUST be for the Highest Good of All involved.

Even if it doesn't particularly feel like it right now. But we will continue holding the vision.

September 29:

After yesterday's disappointing news, a magickal friend gifted me a bear rib and a piece of carnelian crystal to lift my Spirits.

This rental market is incredibly competitive right now. I have never *not* be able to rent a place before. As John Lennon sang, *"Strange days indeed, Mama"*.

I choose to remind myself that which I seek, is also seeking me.

I look forward to discovering "it" one day soon!

September 30:   **BLACK MOON**
(SECOND NEW MOON THIS MONTH)

★ NEW MOON. NEW CYCLE. NEW INTENTIONS.
BLACK MOON: SECOND NEW MOON IN THE SAME CALENDAR MONTH.
THIS ONE HAS SOME EXTRA MAGICK MOJO.

- WHAT ARE MY LONG TERM GOALS FOR THE NEXT TWO YEARS?
- WHAT ABOUT FIVE YEARS FROM NOW?
- AM I HEADING IN THE RIGHT DIRECTION?
- HOW DO I WANT TO FEEL IN THIS COMING MOON CYCLE?
- WHAT ARE MY PRIORITIES TO ACCOMPLISH?
- WHAT IS MY PLAN?

These days I feel as though I am navigating a tight corner in a dense fog.

When I'm approaching an s-bend in my car, I don't slam on the brakes. I reduce my speed and maneuver the turn with due diligence. I am determined to allow whatever is unfolding. I am choosing to hold trust.

When I feel my trust beginning to slip, I will call upon my Highest Self, all my Angels and all my Messengers and ask them for assistance.

I commit to not doing anything impulsive that may thwart my unfolding. I will confidently continue in the direction of my dreams because that's where I want to go. Not back.

My priority is to continue building Spirit Spoon stock inventory for the craft fair. To continue promoting my offerings, and continue in small imperfect actions that continue to bring me closer to that goal.

Online orders have begun being received for Spirit Spoons and my "She Grows" booklet. I am incredibly excited and grateful to be sending them out!

October
2016

"SEEDS ON THE AUTUMN WIND"

October 1:

Saging myself before I headed out, I moved beyond fear or hesitation today "confidently" introducing myself as the Grateful Goblin at a Self Employed Women's conference. I felt self-doubt lurking in my mind on the drive into town for the tradeshow. Instead of reasoning with it in an effort to dismiss it, I stood my ground, telling it assertively *"not today- I don't even have time for you!"* I think I caught it off guard. Normally, I'd have arm wrestled with it, and we (self-doubt and I) would have a strange bond for a moment, instead, it seemed snubbed, turned, and left with no further comment. I'm going to have to remember that approach!

At the conference I commissioned a poem from an entrepreneurial ten year old burgeoning poetess. "What do you want it to be about?" she asked me, and I knew immediately, "being brave!" I smiled at the opportunity to encourage her creativity.

October 2:

Upon their return from a DaddyMan weekend one of My Little Roommates announces:

"I learned this weekend I'd be perfectly happy playing guitar on the back of a hayride tractor for a living."

The saucy sibling chirps up from the backseat, "Well, that'll get you through part of the year".

I am grateful they are including their happiness as a factor while considering their future aspirations.

October 3:

A couple of weeks ago a friend asked if I would help by driving their daughter into school each morning. In our new communal living situation, time with just the three of us is a rarity. Our time in the car has been our opportunity to speak freely and express anything that has been bothering us. As much as I had wanted to help, after driving the girl in for a number of weeks it is proving to be more of a stretch given that I already feel overextended. I was able to express to my beautiful friend and she understood where I was coming from.

Martyrdom comes in many different forms. I don't like it when I default back to a place of *"woe is me- look at all I do for everybody"*. I am responsible for all I do, and for all the times I put others ahead of my own well being. I am learning to do things differently; to keep myself at the top of my priorities. I am grateful for learning opportunities and healthy boundaries. I am grateful for understanding friends.

What distractions am I piling onto my plate of life? Is it stuff that I absolutely love and will savour and enjoy? Or am I making myself eat something I don't like?

I give myself permission to clear it into the proverbial compost.

October 4:

The four of us: My Little Roommates, dog, and myself curled up in the Magick Attick. Snuggling and laughing in my bed like a tangled knot of wiggling puppies. I want to take this memory, and fold it deep within my heart.

This is love.

This is family.

Crazy freaking grateful.

October 5:

Most of the plants in my garden have begun to wither and prepare for dormancy. But the last of my dahlias continue to bloom. Looking at the clenched buds hoping to unfold, I wonder if they will have the opportunity to open before overnight frost claims their efforts. Or perhaps they will bloom for us before we find home?

Venturing out to clip them and bring them inside, the tiniest spider had built her web between the stems, and so I opted to let the flowers stand.

Messaging a friend tonight that we didn't get the rental place, his first response is, "I guess that means something even better is coming".

So deeply grateful for friends that can keep the hope alive when it feels as though mine has wilted on the vine, much like that dwindling garden out back.

October 6:

Life with children is never boring, and I am grateful for the adventure. "I am writing out my 'Gratefuls', and you doing the breakdance move 'the worm' on the foot of my bed isn't helping me write".

October 7:

As I am in the middle of a yawn one of My Little Roommate bellows "You know Mom, I'm sick of your attitude!" she always makes me laugh.

October 8:

As I locked up the house on this grey and drizzly morning raindrops cling to an Autumn spider web outside our back door. Along the highway great spun cobweb chandeliers hang from telephone poles and overhead power lines in a near haunted looking mist. I love this time of year.

October 9:

Somewhere floating around this house is a page of gratefuls I started this morning. I admit I love discovering half started pages of gratefuls. Appearing out of nowhere from days before like wildflowers blooming from seeds scattered on an Autumn wind.

October 12:

"I sure am grateful you moved up into the Magick Attick with me and your sister from two levels down." I tell My Little Roommate, "You felt so far away down there. I missed you."

She smiles "I was just thinking that yesterday! I'm really glad too!"

Thumpity thump thump
Thumpity thump thump
Beats my grateful, grateful heart.

A friend commented tonight how she is envious of our circumstance. All three of us basically sharing bedrooms in an open space without walls. I wonder if one day we will look back, and reminisce about our time together: elbow to elbow.

Love Bubbles to all.

October 13:

Sometimes the things people say without thinking before they speak blows me away.

"It must be nice to have that kind of time" a cashier said snidely to me today regarding my self-care and hiking. The good news is, it allowed me the opportunity to demonstrate to My Little Roommates how to let an ignorant comment bounce off of me.

Opinion flags flapping in the wind.
Opinion flags flapping in the wind.

Opinion flags flapping in the wind.

I will not gift wrap my personal power and slide it across to the bearer of snarky opinions in way of my reaction.

Later today, one of My Little Roommates remarked about the exchange. I am being watched, and they learn by my example. I am grateful of being mindful of this and for the opportunity to demonstrate being non-reactive. Thank you dear person for allowing me this opportunity by way of your remarks.

October 14:

The wind howls and rain pelts against the window as I sit in bed by candlelight during a power outage recording today's gratefuls. I love the sound of rain falling onto the slanted roof overhead. I am grateful I listened to my Intuition earlier: doing as much laundry as I could, and cooking dinner earlier in anticipation of a possible power outage. My Little Roommates and I ate dinner with just our fingers in the dark. Our meal laid out across a large upholstered ottoman. A small battery operated lantern hanging overhead. Indoor picnic in the dark.

October 15:   FULL HUNTER'S MOON

★ FULL MOON REFLECTIONS:

- HAVE MY FEELINGS AND EMOTIONS BEEN CONSISTENT WITH WHAT I DECLARED AS MY NEW MOON INTENTIONS?
- WHAT NEEDS TO BE SHIFTED?
- WHAT WILL I DELEGATE TO ANOTHER?
- HOW WILL I ASK FOR SUPPORT?

This afternoon My Little Roommate and I stood on the end of the Roberts Creek pier. Arm in arm, hand in hand, for more than an hour. Laughing and hollering as an extravagantly powerful wind and rain storm barrelled down upon us. We stood there until our clothing was absolutely drenched. Our faces red and stinging from being pelted by the intense rains. Every cell of our beings charged with the screaming vibrations of Mother Nature's forces.

October 16:

Slow going sleepy Sunday morning curled up in in our wee living room space watching a movie. I savour my coffee slowly. Cozy blankets. Dog snuggled in amongst the three of us. My heart marinades in gratitude.

October 17:

I miss my Full Moon sheet changing ritual: hanging them on a clothesline overnight beneath the moonlight. But I continue as best I can with what I have. I think of the snake who doesn't look back mournfully over shedded skin left in her wake. An old friend used to say, "Die. Adjust. Or Migrate."

(((Grateful)))

October 18:

With the craft fair date growing imminently closer I've decided to temporarily release the search for "home" until January 1st. I can't imagine having to move my stock in addition to all of my household belongings. Pausing in what feels deflated surrender. Resigned that we'll be celebrating Winter Solstice here instead of "home". I allow myself that moment of pause and release, but I will not be defeated, and for that tenacious Warrior Goddess Spirit, I am grateful.

October 19:

Curled up in bed in the darkness when I realized I hadn't recorded my day's gratitude. Sat up, light on, writing. I am grateful I didn't break the chain.

October 20:

Cohabitating with an ex-boyfriend is a *strange* dynamic. It's not as if I can easily date. Things I didn't take into consideration when we merged houses. It has been a long seven months. I got brave today and told someone I have feelings for him. Well. As brave as one can be, when you wait until there is a vast body of water between you and the object of your affection. But still: I admitted to my feelings. I exposed myself. Well.... Not *that* way. I am grateful for my bravery and vulnerability.

October 21:

I challenged a lot of beliefs and stories today and took a lot of bold courageous imperfect actions in the direction of my dreams. I am incredibly grateful for continued bravery.

October 22:

Dinner time conversation in the Ocean of Estrogen,

"Are you sure you won't date women?" one of them asks casually.

Her saucy sister chirps in with an eye roll, "I've been encouraging that for months. I don't think she's budging".

Hearty laughter overflowed the kitchen table and fills our makeshift kitchen. I am grateful for young open minds, candid conversations, and the laughter we share.

October 23:

Last night was filled with nightmares re-experiencing memories of childhood sexual abuse. I wake up sweaty. My heart racing, my stomach nauseous and the taste of bile rising above a clenched throat. Swinging my legs onto the floor, I have to take immediate action to ground and centre; anchoring myself in the present and deflate the lingering Energy from the experience. This feeling is **not** welcome to stay with me throughout my day. It is not coming with me. I will not spill my Energy everywhere and react to this trigger. I will not allow my day to continue emitting this vibration.

What are three things I can see?

Surveying the Magick Attick I tell myself I see my vision boards hanging on the slanted ceiling above my bed; a tangible reminder of what I want to create and how I want to feel in this Lifetime. On my bedside table I see my Grateful Jar altar. The large turquoise vase near overflowing with folded squares reminding me of all the wonder in my Life. Across from me I see My Little Roommates curled up in their bed nests sleeping soundly. There is no threat here. I am a grown up now. I am safe.

What are three things I can feel?

To emphasize to myself where I am, I wiggle my toes atop the small rug next to my bed. I feel my pink flannel bedsheets beneath roaming fingertips before I raise my arms overhead to indulge in a long luxurious stretch to release the tension. Inhaling slowly and deeply, I imagine the branches of my lungs as though they are a tree bursting forth from Winter dormancy into a bloom of lush green new growth. Leaves uncurling from buds as I inhale as fully as I can. Exhaling slowly, deeply, I release the stress from the pit of my stomach. It rises and curls like a ribbon of smoke twisting and twirling, exiting my body through my mouth. This apparition of haunting cellular memory is not welcome to lurk in the space of the Magick Attick. I specifically banish it, envisioning it heading towards the open window where it curls through, dissipating into the cool misty Autumn morning.

What are three things I can hear?

I hear birdsong outside the window. I hear the whelps and near giggle sounds of animated puppy dreams at the foot of my bed. I hear the light snoring from one of My Little Roommates... a contented sleepy sigh emerges from one of them.

I breathe. I heal. I learn. I do differently.

Climbing into the shower, I visualize white streams of Light pouring forth from the shower head atop of me. Any remnants of the dream, anything left in my Energy field, being washed off by the flow of water, and circling down the drain.

I am deeply grateful for positive coping skills. Once upon a time, a nightmare like that would have messed me up for days. Possibly weeks. Another progress check point. I wrap my arms around myself in embrace, sending deep, unconditional Love and compassion to myself.

Love Bubbles. Lots and lots and lots of Love Bubbles.

I am an adult. I am safe. I am peace.

I am grateful.

October 24:

One of My Little Roommates returned home from school this afternoon with an advertisement for a small rental cottage. Her teacher was handing out assignments, placed the typed piece of paper on the desk and slid it over to her without saying a word about it.

It is not our ideal of what we are looking for: it is tiny. Only 800 square feet. It is short a bedroom. There is no yard space there would be no garden. It is incredibly remote (I'm actually attracted to that). But I am open to being flexible and compromising.

Really Universe?!?

The power of surrender.

Thank you.

Thank you. Thank you. Thank you. Thank you.

October 25:

I'm on the fence as to whether or not I should pursue the small rental cabin. I don't want to jump from the frying pan into the fire just for the sake of finally getting out of here. My heart hangs heavy at the prospect of no yard. No garden.

Talking to a friend on the telephone today about the quandary she says to me, "Don't dismiss moving before the craft fair just because of the timing. Sure, it'll be hard. But if there's one thing I know about you: you can do hard."

Tonight I am grateful for hope on the horizon, the encouragement of good friends, and tenacity of Spirit. Could this be it I wonder.... Could *this* be it?

October 26:

It should be noted that today's very special gratefuls were recorded on the back of the printed advertisement provided yesterday by a teacher.

We met home today! A tiny 800 square foot carriage house perched atop the landlord's workshop. It has a large master bedroom and a secondary den which we can easily utilize as a bedroom. Though it is tiny it has high raised slanted ceilings with skylights in the main room. My Little Roommates and I carefully negotiate with one another if we can make this work: the two of them can share the master bedroom and I can take the small room. I'm confident my queen size bed will fit in the tiny space though the door may not close. I joke with them that it will ensure open door parenting.

There is no yard. No room to garden. Nowhere to throw the ball for dog. Is this doable: can we all commit to taking turns walking her regularly? There shall be no easy fix of just opening the front door in the morning and letting her wander out to pee. There is only ONE closet. There is no bathtub. This one is tricky: can we do it?

The overall vote was: yes.

I hear a long ago neighbour's voice in my head: *die, adjust or migrate.*

After an arduous and extensive eight month search for home, we will be moving in a mere six days.

What is it this year about swift moves? I pulled the last one off in eight days. This one will be done in six. I will do this one more time.

Thumpity thump thump
Thumpity thump thump
Beats my grateful, grateful heart.

October 27:

Moving preparations are in full force! I am grateful I began collecting cardboard boxes at the end of August.

A great purge is underway given the size of the space we are moving into. This cohabitation experience has greatly influenced my view of belongings, the trappings of "stuff" and the impact of physical environments. With near relief I am scrutinizing and prioritizing our belongings, only that which brings us joy will be joining us in the new space.

A friend of ours owns a thrift store and has been accommodating our significant donations on a regular basis. There is a large fire pit where we have been staying and I have been burning often. If I can't clearly identify the purpose a belonging serves, or where I will keep it, it is being sent to the thrift store or fed to the flames.

There is something most cathartic about releasing with a bonfire.

Without even being asked a brave friend has volunteered to assist with our move. She will bring her son along for extra assistance. Adventure is in the air and cooperation is coming from out of nowhere. I am so deeply grateful.

October 28:

As a credit card free family I am grateful another helpful friend is guaranteeing the U-haul reservation for me with her credit card number. I am really, really grateful for cooperation and generosity of Spirit.

October 29:

This is my last child free weekend living in the Magick Attick.

A friend messages me that my telephone number says it is no longer in service. After borrowing the co-tenant's cell phone, my service provider tells me they misunderstood my requested dis-connection date. They apologized, but warned me that my inter-net was also scheduled for disconnection. They can't reschedule the disconnection on this end without bumping the service instal-lation date at the new address. I was offered a $200 credit for my inconvenience.

For whatever inexplicable reason, the internet didn't disconnect, and I was at least able to message my moving helpers online to solidify moving plans for Wednesday. The credit received for the telephone inconvenience has created some wiggle room to accommodate mov-ing expenses. All is unfolding just as it should. I am once again, as always, being supported by all compassionate all supportive Uni-verse. I am deeply grateful.

October 30:   **NEW MOON**

★ NEW MOON. NEW CYCLE. NEW ENERGIES. NEW INTENTIONS:

- IN THE IMPENDING EXCITEMENT OF OUR MOVE: WHAT IS MY DESIRED EMOTIONAL EXPERIENCE?
- WHAT CAN I DO NOW, TO HELP ELIMINATE SOME OF THE STRESS?

After considering this most of the day, I appreciate that there is no opportunity for take out or delivery in the rural outreaches of where we are moving to. I choose to be proactive in having something quick and easy available for dinner to prevent any hunger related crankiness. Moving is hard enough without a teenager going all "hangry" on you.

As night settled I had the opportunity to chat online with a much younger half sister. I learned my estranged biological father's dying words today. It was a heavy feeling mixed with an interesting observation that I had never once wondered what they had been before today. But I am grateful to have learned they were "I love my kids".

Peace be with you, wherever you are at.

October 31:   **HALLOWE'EN**

The silhouette of My Little Roommate bounding down dark forested driveways. Her swaying pigtails reflecting her confident swagger in a determined pursuit of sugary offerings. Her candy sack clenched in one fist. A borrowed lantern in the other. I am so grateful to witness this enchanted childhood moment.

November
2016

"FLOW DAY"

November 1:

Just the other week I purchased a four kilogram jug of bathtub Epsom salts. Never in a million years thinking I'd be moving into a place with only a walk in shower. I chose to interpret this as a personal self-care challenge and today I managed to use the last of them! I am grateful for challenges met head on, the last of the long hot baths and one less thing to move.

November 2:

After what seemed a never ending search for a rental home, the day is finally here! A dear friend has dubbed it "flow day" instead of "moving day".

Once everything is loaded up into the truck, I say my very strange and strained goodbyes to our co-tenant. I can feel the Energy of Kali-Ma's presence. I realize what I hadn't before: This cohabitation process was a significant part of my clearing and releasing. I had gone back and forth on this relationship so many times; there would be no going back ever again. I came. I saw. I learned much. It's done. I wish him well.

I've driven Uhauls before but never a 26 ft one. Big girl pants are firmly secured in place and pep talks to self are ongoing. Despite many offers I won't let someone step in to do this for me. I'm brave. I'm capable. I got this! I am modelling strong capable independent womanhood to my two Little Roommates.

Loading the dog onto the floor of the truck cab; she isn't particularly impressed by her lack of window seat. The three of us perched hip to hip across the bench seat like birds on a wire. A palpable mix of excitement, possibility and adventure swirl about us in the truck cab as I steer the helm to our new reality.

I am so freaking grateful.

November 3:

One of My Little Roommates has a field trip today that she has been chattering about excitedly for months. Actually, years! Ever since she first heard about "We Day" concerts, a special inspirational production held for the 'leaders of tomorrow'. It is off coast in the big city, and the stadium doors are closed to entry after 9am. Long story short, the attendees from our area need to be on an early ferry, and given the travel time the school bus is leaving at 4:50am. Just what a weary body wants to accommodate the day after an arduous move!

We arrive late and miss the bus. You can imagine the sense of panic taking hold in my passenger. Taking off driving down the highway in hot pursuit of the school bus, flashing my high beams over and over once we caught up to it. Man, am I grateful the driver had mercy and pulled over for us!

November 4:

To celebrate home we roam pantless and free!!

Standing in the bright living room I realize I recognize this space. The dream I had this summer where all of our stuff was in boxes and I was showing a friend our new place. **This** is the living room from that dream! I didn't recognize it before now. Goosebumps, from head to toe!

Long may it be the power of three: grateful, grateful, grateful.

November 5:

Today I am grateful for the opportunity to unpack, to shift, sort and settle. The ability to have a kitchen to myself again. To be able to organize it!

Dog is getting used to the new space. She thinks the sound of the refrigerator icemaker is the devil incarnate, and she has spent the last two nights barking defensively at her reflection in the kitchen skylight overhead. But again, this too shall pass, we are home, and we are settling. Finally!

November 6:

There is no yard space in our new abode, so everyone is walking the dog far more often. We are discovering nearby meadows and fields where we can have her off leash to throw the ball for her. I was in a field playing ball with her this morning, and two bald eagles circled overhead in an intricate dance, looping and swooping. Gradually, the swoops became lower and lower. I was awestruck being able to see the feathered details of their underbelly overhead.

I am grateful for the truly spectacular feathered spectacle.

November 7:

A dear helpful friend generously went out of her way to borrow a pickup truck to help me transport My Little Roommates bicycles and other miscellaneous outdoor items not included in the truck on "flow day". Blessed be the helpers: I am so *very* grateful.

November 8:

It never fails to amaze me some of the neat things that come to be through social media. From seemingly out of nowhere, I have had the opportunity to participate in a learning astrology group recently started by a very generous astrologer. I have been learning much about birth charts, creation charts, and characteristics of the specific astrological houses. I am grateful for her generosity of Spirit and the sharing of her knowledge.

November 9:

"Mama" she says with great dramatic influx, "I am about to blow your mind." Pointing to the skylight overhead and instructs, "Look up!"

There, perfectly centred within the glass window pane, hung the luminescent beauty of the waxing third quarter moon. I am SO grateful to be able to see Mother Moon from inside our new nest. It is amazing the level of comfort that can be found in the tiny blessings.

November 10:

After dropping My Little Roommates at school I indulge in a quiet walk along the beach on a drizzly grey November morning. Berm and bog on one side of the gravel trail. On the other side churning waves send washed up logs crashing upon the shoreline. Squawking gulls circle overhead. I love the stormy sky reflected in the grey hue of the ocean's surface. The ocean has as many moods as we do. I affectionately refer to my family as the Ocean of Estrogen for a reason.

November 11:

I hold a heavy heart tonight upon hearing of the passing of a friend. The news came delayed, having discovered it several weeks after her death. As I light a candle for her memory and journey, I remind myself I can focus on my frustration that no one told me or I can focus on the Love I had for this woman. Though my mind may be a random thought generator, I hold the ultimate power in which thoughts I will hold and which thoughts I will release.

Tonight I am grateful that this beautiful spirited woman has been freed from a lengthy painful physical struggle. Peace be with you Dear One. You will be, and are, very much missed.

November 12:

The list of "responsible things" I could have been doing, possibly *should have* been doing after last week's move was long and looming large.

I could have, perhaps should have, been unpacking boxes.

I could have, perhaps should have, been organizing a kitchen, or a dresser, or a closet.

I could have, perhaps should have, been preparing for "Spirit Spoons" craft fair debut.

I have an allergic reaction to "you should". It's terrible. I swell up all puffy and my defiant streak of 'you can't tell me what to do' flares up like an unyielding rash.

There comes a point, where we have to claim time for ourselves, lest we end up 'serving time'. Yes, my to-do list is extensively grandiose, and I am overwhelmed just looking at it. Which makes it even more critical for me to take care of myself and my Spirit in this over-whelmed moment.

I headed straight for the boxes labelled *"art supplies"* and tore into them with great gusto and played. I didn't play "to make". I didn't play "to sell". I didn't play with any attachment as to what would emerge. I played for myself. I played for the sheer expression. I played for the pure joy. I took care of myself first so that I could bet-ter care for those I Love.

Tonight I am so grateful I made the time to play, to splash colour about and make a great unruly creative mess. It was fabulous!!!

November 13:

I am grateful for lazy 'pants optional' weekends. No obligations. No expectations. Absolutely nowhere to be, but here in my heart, with My Little Roommates, mastering the perfectly imperfect art of sim-ply being.

On the way home last night, we were driving on a dark and winding unlit rural highway and out of nowhere I speak aloud, "I'd like to just take a minute and thank all of the woodland critters for staying off of the highway and out of our car's path."

Just as I finish the sentiment we come around a bend. My head-lights reflect, glowing in a raccoon's eyes on the side of the highway. Slowly and dramatically pulling his front left paw in a step back-wards from crossing, as though he heard my warning and decided to rethink his approach.

"Whoa!" one of My Little Roommates gasps in amazement from the front passenger seat, "How'd you do **that!?**"

I am grateful for Intuition spoken aloud and serendipitous timing making me look good.

"Only use the powers for good, Girl Child, only use the powers for good."

Thank you raccoon for making smart choices before trying to cross.

November 14:   **FULL BEAVER MOON**

★ FULL MOON REFLECTIONS:

○ HAVE I BEEN EXPERIENCING THE EMOTIONS I DESIRED AT THE TIME OF THE NEW MOON?

○ WHERE DO I WANT TO GO FROM HERE?

○ HOW WILL I SPECIFICALLY RECOGNIZE I AM ON THE RIGHT TRACK?

After what has seemed like weeks of rain I stood out on the soaked deck savouring the Full Moon and the darkness. An orchestra of frogs ribbiting and croaking in the background. On night's like these enchantment hangs tangibly in the air. I am deeply grateful.

November 15:

I walk dog early this morning when the rest of the neighbourhood is likely still wiping encrusted sleep from the corners of their eyes. Mist clings to tree topped mountain peaks. So many shades of grey it looks more like a watercolour painting created with a limited palette. We walk in silence, dog and I. She sniffs one thousand sniffs, and I watch the sky slowly, sleepily, consider unfolding into daybreak.

November 16:

I overheard one of My Little Roommates' delight this afternoon setting up a display of her crystals.

"They're home! They're home!" she squeals, "They came out a couple of times. They shrugged and thought 'This must be it'. But it wasn't it."

Leaning close to the wall shelf she's perching them on she whispers, "*This* is it!".

My heart swells overflowing as I watch the sweet sight of watching them both nest. Beaming.

Thumpity thump thump
Thumpity thump thump
Beats my grateful, grateful heart.

November 17:

I was reminded today of the power of incorporating root chakra work (or in layman's terms: masturbation) in raising and harnessing manifesting Energy. This womb and these tender bits of mine have the potential to nourish the spark that brings forth new creation. I am grateful for the reminder! This is a no shame zone. This is my body that houses my Soul, and there is no room for anything less than magick. I'm also grateful for orgasms. They're freaking awesome.

November 18:

Feeling anxiety nearing, I imagine it approaches me as though it were on a grocery store conveyor belt. When the item reaches the cashier to be electronically scanned, they don't just stop and clutch the item. It comes to them, they scan it, and they release it. They do not hold it in a clenched state unwilling to release.

"To me...with me...away from me" I remind myself. I am grateful for both the mantra and the visualization. I am releasing anxiety as it arises: to me, briefly with me, away from me.

I breathe.

November 19:

The smell of forest. The crunch of each step. Laughter. One-on-one time. Uninterrupted. Bliss. I am grateful for two hours in the forest with dog and one of My Little Roommates and not a single other person to be seen.

November 20:

A quiet moment with one of My Little Roommates before retiring to bed. Working together to help identify our "gratefuls" for the day. I love it when they share their perspectives with me. Watching them twisting and turning their soulful kaleidoscopes in pursuit of their own bright side.

November 21:

Sister Sledge's "We Are Family" comes on the radio and is followed by Tragically Hip's "Lil Bones". My conversation with the playful

Universe continues. Unfolding in its cryptic nature. Still. Always. This time through a radio DJ's synchronistic playlist.

I am incredibly grateful to call these girls my family.

I am surrounded by Love and vibrancy.

I am incredibly grateful to know home again.

Crazy freaking grateful. Blessings and Love Bubbles to that DJ in his little radio booth.

Love Bubbles to all.

November 22:

Upon waking I am grateful for last night's deep restful slumber. Before I get out of bed, I lay there taking a quiet moment in my warm blanketed cocoon. Savouring the sound of the rainstorm outside. Rainstorms always sound far more delicious when you aren't standing ankle deep in them. I am grateful for this dry toasty peaceful moment before I embark to walk dog in the torrential downpour.

November 23:

My Little Roommate awoke this morning to discover her sister curled up in her bed beside her. She had scrambled into join her in the middle of the night in response to a crane wailing outside. "It sounded like a woman screaming" she explains earnestly. As grateful as I am they have one another to take comfort in, I am equally grateful I miraculously remained the sole inhabitant of my bed last night.

November 24:

I am grateful for the realization that thinking about life decisions at bedtime is a bad idea. Noted!

Conveyor belt time. To me. With me. Away from me.

Hey- look! Off, off, off it glides.

(((Grateful)))

November 25:

Tonight I baked with my grandmother's vintage metal measuring spoons. I imagine her standing by my side donning her apron, just like she would have when I was a little girl, supervising accurate measurements of the sugar, salt and baking powder. Her hand over mine, gripping the wooden spoon, mixing the ingredients together with me.

Our tiny cottage glows with soft light from crystal lamps. Soon it will be filled with the aroma of freshly baked cookies. I am deeply grateful for the nostalgia swirling about and the enchanted coziness of home.

Thank you Life. I love you.

November 26:

I've recognized that when the organ grinding Monkey Mind partner is tripping out I can **opt out** of the illusion that **IS** Monkey Mind to begin with. This has been a big BIG lesson. Huuuuuge!

I wonder if I could bottle this. An opt out repellent. Carry it in my purse or my coat pocket.

I am grateful for self-awareness, mindfulness, and playfully using my imagination to opt out of internal dramas.

November 27:

I am practicing not feeling overwhelmed with my to-do list and all that has to be done in time for next weekend's craft fair. Rummaging through drawers for price stickers I stumble across the "Be Brave" poem I bought back in September from a young poetess.

I have been navigating the paradox of my Inner Artist not wanting to be seen. I have assured her she can stay safely tucked away, finger painting, in the confines of my imagination. I will take care of this. She has nothing to worry about. I can handle this. I am open to allowing and enjoying this experience.

So crazy grateful I stumbled across the "Be Brave" poem today. I send Love Bubbles to the young poetess with a beaming smile spreading across my face.

I got this.

You smell that? It's my Opt Out repellent hanging thick in the air. I'm spraying that stuff *everywhere*!

November 28:

Dog is trying to adjust to our new morning ritual of walking around the neighbourhood in the black darkness. **Trying**. Bless her rescued heart. She is *trying* to leave the anxiety of highway life behind her. But in her heightened hypervigilance she flinches and jumps at every perceived noise.

"There's a monster out there," I hear her panicked fretting in my imagination, *"it follows my every step. This creature lurking in the shadows. I can't outrun it, it matches my pace! I try to let it pass when I pause to sniff, but this demon of the darkness is relentless in its pursuit!"*

"Yea, um, that's me.... holding your leash. I'd have thought me clutching the bag of your feces would have been the first clue".

"No. I thought, first, it bagged my poop, and then it would bag my soul".

Tonight I am grateful for the comical adventures of life with a worried dog. I am so grateful for all she brought into our world with her quirks and characteristics. I am grateful for the opportunity to provide her with a safe and loving home environment.

November 29:   NEW MOON

★ New Moon. New Energy. New Cycle. New Intentions:

- Do I know where I want to go from here?
- How do I want to feel in the coming weeks as the moon grows full?
- What are my priorities to be accomplished?

I am excited by the craft fair coming up soon. It is the next piece of my unfolding jigsaw puzzle, I can feel it in my bones. I am curious to sift, sort and shuffle to see where this piece of the puzzle fits and what it will expand.

Interestingly enough now that I am home I somehow feel less connected to my Grateful Jar Project. It was the life jacket that kept me buoyant through the trials and tribulations of this stormy year. Now that I am seemingly on stable dry land I want to stop wearing it and be done with it. Being so close to the completion of this project I instead shrug out of my resistance. This has been an intense year and I have so much to be grateful for. It is important to me that the Universe know it has not gone unnoticed.

Like I did months and months ago in the Magick Attick I mount a sign above my bed. New sign. For a new home and new Energies, "*Have you done your gratefuls?*" I take the opportunity to create a fresh altar upon my nightstand surrounding the jar with crystals and candles before feeding the table drawer a fresh stash of papers and pens.

Christmas lights have begun popping up through the neighbourhood. I am grateful for the cheerful colours stretching along fences. I am grateful for memories of childhood wonder beginning the countdown to Christmas morning.

As I walk I envision Love Bubbles flowing freely from the crown of my head billowing into the neighbourhood in our wake.

Thank you, Life. Thank you mischievously playful co-creating Universe. Thank you Mother Father Creator. Thank you my 'Beloved I Am Presence'.

Thank you. Thank you. Thank you.

Love Bubbles to all.

November 30:

As I hike this morning I wonder why the forest hasn't whispered to me in the weeks that I've been back. Not even a single stuttered syllable. As I hike farther and farther in I realize: you can't philosophize spiritual truths to a starving person. First, the ravenous hunger has to be satisfied *then* deep conversation can be had. This is what my enchanted forest has been doing these past few weeks for me. Feeding me. Nurturing me. Lovingly tending and mending to my metaphorical scratched knees and scraped elbows. She will speak again soon.

December
2016

"LOVE BUBBLES
AND
GLOWING PUZZLE PIECES"

December 1:

After months of building anticipation tonight is the set up date of my Spirit Spoons table at the craft fair. Since moving I now live an hour away from the location so My Little Roommates are vying to come assist me. Well maybe one of them more than the other. I'm being diplomatically generous here.

They eventually grow bored of watching me set up my nook and opt to catch a bus. Taking the opportunity to venture into Sechelt to do some of their own holiday gift shopping away from my eyes. It is nice being back in an area with access to public transit, if only for one night. A novelty we no longer have access to in Garden Bay. It makes their adventure tonight extra sweet. I'm grateful for the opportunity for them to embark on their independent adventure.

It is rare when everyone's different needs are able to be met and balanced. I savour this special moment.

I will be back in two days to man my table at the craft fair for the weekend. I am excited. I'm equally nervous and terrified but I'm focusing on the excitement.

December 2:

It is a long distance commute to My Little Roommate's school. One that winds past many spectacular sights. We are so enamoured by the beauty that we have developed a good morning ritual. Okay, **I** have developed a good morning ritual over the past month since living here.

"Good morning Ghosties" I say aloud as we meander past the historical Sundowner Inn. Overlooking Hospital Bay the building was once St Mary's Hospital and the site is rumoured to be haunted.

"Good morning lake" I say aloud as we pass the village's aquifer.

"Good morning Ron" I call to the resident heron standing on the lake's edge. I've dubbed him Ron specifically so I can greet him, "Hey- Ron!".

"Good morning Tiger," I call aloud overhead to the large stuffed tiger a resident has perched high on a mossy embankment over the meandering forested road.

"Good morning my dead lovelies. Peace be with you!" I call aloud to the small community graveyard overlooking Oyster Bay below. I say hello and goodbye to them every time we pass.

"Good morning mossy spot..." I greet one of my favourite mossy rocky embankments. Moments later, yet another favourite thick mossy patch "Good morning, mossy spot". Moments later, yet another.

"I love that mossy spot," I gush to My Little Roommate. She pats my leg nearly condescendingly. Replying, "You love *all* mossy spots". With my sights focused on the highway before us, I can't see it, but I can hear the lilt of an eye roll in her intonation.

I am grateful for my good morning ritual. I'm excited for our future! I hold a hopeful heart and give thanks for all the amazing things on their way to us that I don't have a clue about as of yet!

Just like Life, and the winding s-bends of the highway before me: I don't know what is around the corner. But I trust I am safe. I know I have the ability to navigate whatever presents.

December 3:

First day of the weekend long craft fair today!

My table is above the main floor roosted upon the community hall stage. There are only three booths up here. I am grateful to be above the throng of attendees that from my glance look crammed in elbow to elbow. The booth next to me has a large tapestry of Buddha hanging above the jewelry display which does an excellent job of drawing attention to us.

At some point during the day a casual acquaintance asked me for an unusually large favour. Once upon a time, as a previous 'co-dependent people pleaser', I'd have put my own needs and responsibilities to the side in order to accommodate the request. At which point I would complete my role as the martyr by brewing and stewing in resentment over what I had done for them. I remind myself martyrdom comes in many different forms and I'm no longer participating in *any* of them. So when I was presented with this imposition I recognized it as an opportunity to practice saying no without offering *any* explanation.

I am learning new ways. For that I am grateful.

<u>December 4:</u>

Second day of the craft fair. I remind myself that if I choose to participate again next year I will find a place to stay overnight so I don't have an hour commute each way. In fact I have a page titled "Notes To Self" for 2017 craft fairs recording my observations and what I may consider doing differently next year.

For months I have known that there would be someone pivotal I was going to meet at this craft fair. I naively assumed it would be a man and it would likely be a romantic relationship.

Tonight upon reflecting, I realize it is in fact the beautifully Spirited woman at the booth next to me. No I am not suddenly attracted to women as My Little Roommates encourage. In her I have met a like minded person and we hold a shared eclectic spirituality in common. I do believe I caught a glowing glimpse of one of the pieces to my puzzle tucked deep in one of her tunic pockets. Throughout the weekend she has offered so many tips, feedback and insight.

As I take down the craft fair display and return home with a pocket and heart full of abundance, I give deep, deep thanks for the magick that sparks when women support one another.

I will water and tend to the new growth of this new acquaintance in the hopes it will one day blossom into friendship. I offer her and all that I encountered this weekend Love Bubbles in my wake as I depart the hall and embark on my journey back home.

December 5:

Knowing that I would be drained after a weekend surrounded by that many people I wisely scheduled myself a couple of days reprieve to accommodate my introvert hangover. When My Little Roommates are at school I spend the day puttering, organizing. Shifting and shuffling. Recharging. Nesting in our new abode.

I tend to play hide and go seek with my belongings. That is code for: I misplace my stuff a lot. But instead of stressing out about it, I try to handle it with childlike wonder, as if I am playing hide and go seek. Instead of stressing that I can't find whatever it is I'm looking for. I call the object aloud by name as though I was calling a pet or a loved one.

Usually the misplaced item will cooperate and come into my view nearly immediately. However I have a stubborn playmate as of late: a painting. I have been calling her name, but I think she has been enjoying the "seek" portion of hide and go seek too much.

Most of the artwork that survived my great purging bonfire in October has already been hung in our tiny home. But I've kept an empty spot on the wall for a specific piece. A piece I haven't been able to find since we moved in. I am perplexed, because how *does* one misplace a 16 x 20 canvas in a space no more than 800 square feet?

Today she finally revealed herself, having been wedged inside the back of another larger canvas. I'm thrilled to have finally found her! I welcomed her to our new home and introduced her to her long awaited spot on the wall. Welcome home, Love, welcome home! Thank you for finally appearing.

December 6:

Having deposited My Little Roommates at their respective schools this morning I took the opportunity to claim a pocket of self-care for myself and headed to the beach.

The weak December sun tries to fill an overcast grey Winter morning. I sit on a driftwood log bundled in warm layers writing out affirmations for magnetizing prosperity and abundance. Savouring the smell of the brine, the sound of crashing surf. Relishing the unexpected treat of gentle sunshine on my face.

Tonight I am grateful for seized opportunities. Quiet moments of peace. I am grateful for the poetry within our five senses. I am grateful for the knowledge that whatever I look for, I will find evidence to support. I am grateful for this marvellous Life, this wonderful body, and all it does for me.

December 7:

Continuing with my life strategist's "do something different challenge" I attend a small meeting tonight with a group of local entrepreneurial women. I am practicing seizing new opportunities that I feel are in alignment with what I want to create in my Life.

During the meeting I'm trying to pay attention to the speaker but I am distracted by the flashes of Light emerging as though playing peek-a-boo with me from the upright piano standing behind her.

When the meeting ends and the attendees have departed, I say to the hostess, "You have quite the mischief maker here."

"What do you mean?" she asks curious. I risk sounding like a crazy person. But for one reason or another, I took the chance.

"I mean, I kept getting distracted by a Spirit and the piano."

Her face lights up with surprise and she begins to tell me the story of how the piano came into her possession from the community hall. Going on to tell me about a woman who was a fixture for years sitting on the piano bench tickling the ivories. She takes a painting off its perch atop the piano, and shows me a photograph of the woman tucked within the canvas frame.

I am grateful that I not only took the chance, but that I received validation, I mean, *that* could have been awkward.

December 8:

As of today my pyrographed Spirit Spoons are now available for purchase in a local cafe and gift shop. I reflect on where I was last December. Working part time in the pursuit of someone else's dream. If you had told me then that this time next year I'd be selling wooden spoons I refer to as fully functional magick wands for the kitchen, I'd have thought you were trying to pull one over on me. I am grateful for all that has transpired, all the inspirations, all the bold sometimes crazy choices, that have contributed to my experience this year. I give thanks to that fallen tree and the mysterious Monopoly house that seems like eons ago.

December 9:

Keeping on with the "do something different challenge" I opt to do something I've never done before. When My Little Roommates attended youth group in town. I went to bingo. I won $20 on a fly-swatter game! Here's to stepping beyond comfort zones and winning $20!

December 10:

My Little Roommate stresses, "I don't know why you're getting mad at me?"

Me: "What??? Did someone just come into the room and get all angry and I missed it???"

She LAUGHS.

Deflection. Phew! I am grateful.

December 11:

I set the coffee machine to brew this morning before heading out with dog on an early morning walk. The snow covered neighbourhood is reminiscent of a winter scene in a fairytale. Dog and I walk slower than usual as she sticks her snout deep into each snowy paw print, dramatically sniffing and snorting. I practice patience, or try to as I anticipate the delight of aromatic freshly brewed coffee awaiting me in the tiny warm cottage.

"C'mon Bella... Coffee..." she tilts her head and looks up at me and I in my imagination I hear her speak in my mind *"But I still don't know the colour of the dog's eyes that peed here three Wednesdays ago".*

I am grateful for being smart enough to set the coffee up to brew in our absence. The anticipation of freshly brewed coffee. Dog sniffing one thousand snow covered sniffs. It seems to be smelly grateful list today.

December 12:

Piling into the car this dark morning to embark upon our great journey to their various schools. When I turn the key in the ignition the great dramatic "Carmina Burana" opera bursts to life. Pouring through car speakers at top volume. As I quickly turn it down, My Little Roommate wittily chirps up from the backseat. "Inquiring,"

"Are we going into battle?!?"

Poor timing. Having just taken a sip from my travel mug, I spurt hot coffee throughout the interior of the car in response to her dry humour. Sometimes that's how gratitude presents: sprayed across the inside of the car windshield, all over the dash, and down the front of me.

My heart overflows with happy emotions. Grateful for being privileged enough to transport them everyday during this strange year of transition. Pride at my commitment to follow through on my word. To have made the daily sacrifice: to absorb the expense and rearrange daily life to accommodate the travel.

I am grateful for the gift of family time during this extended commute. Time free from internet or text messages. But most of all, I am grateful for the conversations we have during this time. How often they make me laugh in these moments.

Even if I have to mop coffee off of my dashboard.

December 13:   FULL COLD MOON

★ FULL MOON REFLECTIONS:

- ○ WHERE AM I IN THE PURSUIT OF GOALS SET THIS TIME LAST YEAR?
- ○ WHAT ACCOMPLISHMENTS ARE CELEBRATION WORTHY?

This time last year I knew I yearned to become self employed. To eke a livelihood from my creations.

I reflect on how Spirit Spoons came to be during a trying year. How "She Grows" emerged as my means of coping through creative expression. I think of the sage bundles I wrapped from harvest that I cultivated from seeds.

This time last year I had barely dared to dream of fusing magick with coaching to create a Wheel of the Year centred platform. I am proud that my New Moon Intentions and Full Moon Reflections have been the beginning of that foundation.

While I did not expect any of this to come about in the ways that it did, I am beyond grateful I dared to listen to the promptings of my Intuition. In my scavenger hunt with the Universe I co-created a Life far more reflective of who I am and am utilizing the gifts I have to share with my community.

I am in awe of the opportunities, the lessons presented, and how I navigated them. I dared to rise!

My unfolding continues. Through the rest of my days, my unfolding continues. This is just the very beginning!

Tonight as I lay in bed. Even though I had already recorded my gratitude for the day. I was compelled to sit. To turn on a bedside lamp, and rewrite them in the form of a poem....

The rapidly melting snow
Drips from the roof
Sounding like a fast paced metronome
Tapatapatapatapatap.
Rain falls on the skylight
Swishing like a brush grazing a drum
A gust of ocean wind
Rushing in to join the symphony.

She lays next to me, asleep
Cuddled beneath layered blankets
The soft rise and fall of her breath
The hushed lyrics to this full moon song
And my heart pumps its grateful dance.

December 14:

Two elk encounters today. The first one early this morning. A herd of them just standing there in the fog in the middle of the highway. I suspect they were in the process of crossing and stopped upon hearing my car's approach. They are such majestic animals and the recovering city slicker in me is continually amazed seeing this huge noble animal just casually loitering.

Encountered the buck of the herd again this evening. Once again just standing there in the middle of the road at dusk on our way to the school concert. I am grateful for elk encounters and being able to stop safely each time. I'm surprised there aren't more elk hood ornaments out here. Especially if this is where they choose to hang out. I am grateful all were unscathed. Make smart choices, elk. Make smart choices. Help me help you.

December 15:

One of My Little Roommates is inclined to inexplicable gushing nosebleeds. This afternoon driving along the highway, she quickly dives into the glovebox digging for a napkin, a tissue, anything to absorb the spontaneous crimson eruption from her face.

"I summoned another demon, Mama. I can't help it. It just happens."

Tonight I am grateful for the life medicine that is humour, even the dark and twisted kind. *Especially* the dark and twisted kind! I am grateful for legacies of neighbour's sage wisdom and send her Love Bubbles. I am also very grateful there were napkins in that glove box. And the presence of stain remover atop my washing machine at home.

December 16:

For the past week I have been feeling momentum dwindling. On this much anticipated last day of school before Winter Break, I hold ritual to mark the pause and honour ebbing Energies.

On narrow strips of paper I write down the goals I've been working towards. On the back of the slip I name specific actions I will resume after the holidays.

Taking a jar of water collected from the lake, I submerge each slip one at a time. Wishing them well as I deposit the lidless jar into my cube freezer. Giving them the time and the space to hang in suspended animation in Winter dormancy. Much like a lake freezing along its edges, aquatic inhabitants waiting out the cold by burrowing deep within the mud.

When school is back in session I will retrieve the jar. Allow the chunk to melt and reconnect with my projects.

December 17:

Intense and inexplicable sadness washed over me suddenly in a grocery store tonight. This feeling is not mine: I am not in it. Looking around I can't help but wonder whose emotions I just walked through. Clueless I decide to observe the emotion with detached curiosity. I imagine the sound of the imaginary grocery store conveyor belt bringing this emotional experience closer and closer.

"Oh, hello angst. How nice of you to join me for a while."

As though angst were a squirming cantankerous toddler, I bend down lifting him up beneath his armpits. I do not plan on holding this flailing angstful emotional experience for long.

To me.

Briefly with me.

Away from me.

Placing him seated on the conveyor belt. I wave animatedly to him. Wishing him a bon voyage as he is carried farther and farther and farther away from me in his continued temper tantrum state.

Breathing deeply I imagine tree roots once again emerging from beneath the arches of my feet. Stretching deep into the centre of the earth to ground me.

I am grateful for the many teachers I've known in my lifetime. Teachers that have imparted their unique insights in my quest of emotional intelligence. I am grateful for the powers of imagination and visualization. For the hard earned insights of self-awareness and mindfulness. To be able to observe the washing over of intense emotions without acting upon them. Just as mysteriously as they suddenly appear they too will disappear in their own time. Until they dissipate I observe the feelings with detachment. Choosing not to hook into them.

December 18:

Dusk closes in and a waning half moon hangs in the sky above. One of My Little Roommates and I are returning from a day of running errands in town. She asks if we can divert and ride the swings at a nearby elementary school. I'm happy to turn off the highway and claim a spontaneous moment of play. Just her and I. The two of us swing higher and higher, hair billowing around our faces, laughter carrying throughout the darkness.

December 19:

It's been a strange Winter of record snowfalls on the Sunshine Coast this year. The house we moved into sits atop a particularly steep gravel driveway which doesn't make shovelling (or traversing the lengths of it) the easiest endeavour in the world. Having awoken this morning to yet another dump of unexpected snow I am especially grateful that I travelled the length of the coast *yesterday*. Errands are completed! Today I am free to sit with a knit blanket draped over my shoulders relaxing in a cozy warm house watching the tranquil beauty through the window.

December 20:

"Did you know in the middle of last night you sat up in your sleep, looked at me, and told me you loved me?" one of My Little Roommates announces.

"I did?" the other replies surprised.

"You did. It was *really* sweet".

What an honour it is to witness the unfolding relationship between these two.

December 21:   WINTER SOLSTICE

The neighbourhood has a sleepy feel as I walk dog this morning. Savouring pink sunlight slowly rising over the mountain top and beginning to spread across the sky. I deeply inhale the lingering aroma of wood smoke rising from a nearby chimney. A rooster sounds his call from across the peninsula and carries across the bay. I briefly think of Alfonso From Afar and realize how long it has been since he has even crossed my mind. Love Bubbles to that rooster and while I'm at it Love Bubbles to the previous co-tenant.

Love Bubbles to all.

My Little Roommates are preparing to again embark on their holiday visit With DaddyMan. I am excited to dive deep into my Soulful Solstice Strategizing. To allow myself to dream. Becoming crystal clear on my desired experience for the coming year; to begin to establish an outline of my plan.

This afternoon as Solstice dinner roasts in the oven I unloaded the contents of the Grateful Jar onto a tabletop. Hundreds and hundreds of folded paper squares spread out before me. My emotions are a mix of excitement, deep thanks, and sense of closure. It has been a dramatic year of powerful flux. As much as I want to celebrate the culmination of the project, I am also eager to put the year behind me. Moving onto the next step that is the unfolding stairwell of my journey.

"What are you going to do with them?" one of My Little Roommates asks me.

Honestly I hadn't even thought about that. What I did know was that before I did anything more I had to put them in chronological order. They had been freed from the jar in a hodgepodge order and I wanted the opportunity to sit in reflection. To read through them in a logical and linear timeline.

It took me hours to unfold each folded square. Laughing at some of the recorded remarks pausing to read the family comedies aloud to My Little Roommates. When I had finished smoothing the folded creases of each page the stack of papers containing my year's worth of gratitude stood close to four inches tall.

Reading through my entries, all of the many twists, turns and unexpected developments it feels as though I have crammed many years in these past 365 days.

Closing Ceremony

Christmas Eve. Midnight, standing in the modest patch of yard I share. I speak in a hushed voice so as not to draw attention from the neighbourhood as I softly fan the flames of a small fire.

"Thank you Mother Father Creator for All this Life lived thus far. Thank you for All my learning that has emerged from many moments of contrast. Thank you for All of my teachers and messengers and growth. Thank you for All the awesomeness that awaits me, that as of this moment, I still know nothing about."

"I give thanks to the North, and the East, and the South, and the West. I give thanks to Mother Earth beneath my feet, Father Sky above, the Waters and Airs of Life. I give thanks to the Sun, and the Moon, and the billions of stars shining down upon us All."

"I give thanks to All of the animals, and All of the Elementals, and All of our Ancestors and All our relations. I give thanks to my parents, my portals into this world, the first catalysts of my learning."

"Thank you Brilliant Light, thank you Darkest of Shadows. Thank you Fear, thank you Love. Thank you...mighty All in All."

Stirring the flames, I speak again, extending my large, now empty turquoise Grateful Jar before me.

"Behold, my Grateful Jar, and All the 'gratefuls' that have flowed to us, around us, and away from us."

I feed my pages of 'gratefuls' to the flames. One month at a time. Pausing, eyes welling with awe, savouring the exquisite heat as my 'gratefuls' are consumed by the flames, transforming into clouds of smoke. Rising, twisting, writhing a curling dance into the night sky.

When I first met that glass turquoise jar, perched high upon a dusty thrift store shelf. I had no inkling the sojourn we would embark on.

> Thumpity thump thump
> Thumpity thump thump
> Beats my grateful, grateful, heart.

Universal Laws

Law of Mentalism: We are all physical embodiments of One Mental Energy. We are all interconnected.

> *"The ALL is Mind; The Universe is Mental."*
>
> *~ The Kybalion.*

Law of Vibration: As beings of Energy we are constantly emitting a vibrational charge. Like Energy attracts like Energy.

> *"Nothing rests; everything moves; everything vibrates."*
>
> *~ The Kybalion.*

Law of Polarity: Everything has two aspects; there are always distinct and direct opposites.

> *"Everything is Dual; everything has poles; everything has its pair of opposites; like and unlike are the same; opposites are identical in nature, but different in degree; extremes meet; all truths are but half-truths; all paradoxes may be reconciled."*
>
> *~ The Kybalion*

Law of Correspondence: Everything corresponds. Whatever we look for we will find evidence to support.

> *"As above, so below; as below, so above."*
>
> *~ The Kybalion.*

Law of Rhythm: Everything has its own season, its own cycle, an ebb and flow.

> *"Everything flows, out and in; everything has its tides;*
> *all things rise and fall; the pendulum-swing manifests in*
> *everything; the measure of the swing to the right is the mea-*
> *sure of the swing to the left; rhythm compensates."*
>
> ~ *The Kybalion.*

Law of Cause and Effect: There is a cause and reaction to everything.

> *"Every Cause has its Effect; every Effect has its Cause;*
> *everything happens according to Law; Chance is but a*
> *name for Law not recognized; there are many planes of*
> *causation, but nothing escapes the Law."*
>
> ~ *The Kybalion.*

Law of Mental Gender: Everything has male and feminine Energies. Our conscious mind is the masculine, the subconscious feminine. Further, every manifestation has its own unique gestational period. It cannot be thwarted or rushed.

> *"Gender is in everything; everything has its Masculine and*
> *Feminine Principles; Gender manifests on all planes."*
>
> ~ *The Kybalion.*

New Moon Intentions and Full Moon Reflections

If you are new to working with the ebb and flow of the moon, a simple Google search will tell you the dates of the various moon phases. If you would like to explore setting your own intentions, here are the journal prompts that are a key component of my Wheel of the Year coaching platform.

★ NEW MOON INTENTIONS:

- WHAT EMOTIONS DO YOU WANT TO FEEL THROUGH THE NEXT FEW WEEKS OF THE LUNAR CYCLE?

- WHAT WILL YOU DO TO GENERATE THOSE EMOTIONS?

- GIVE YOURSELF PERMISSION TO IDENTIFY AND ADMIT TO YOURSELF WHAT IT IS YOU REALLY WANT.

- WHAT ARE YOUR PRIORITIES OVER THE NEXT COUPLE OF WEEKS?

- IS HOW YOU ARE SPENDING YOUR TIME AND INVESTING YOUR ENERGY ALIGNED WITH THE ABOVE?

- HOW WILL YOU SPECIFICALLY ASK FOR ASSISTANCE AND SUPPORT?

- HOW WILL YOU COMMIT TO NURTURING YOURSELF?

- WHAT WILL YOU DELEGATE?

- WHAT ARE YOU GRATEFUL FOR?

★ Full Moon Reflections:

- Have you experienced the emotions set forth as your desired emotional experiences with your new moon intentions?

- Are you being mindful of your thoughts and words? Are you mindfully using these powers for good?

- Have your actions contributed to your desires?

- Are you using your time wisely?

- What distractions have you hooked into?

- Are you enjoying your responsibilities and duties or are you beginning to martyr yourself?

- How will you commit to nurturing yourself?

- What do you give yourself permission to release and clear?

- What will you say no to?

- What progress can you celebrate at this time?

- What are you grateful for?

About the Author

An independent parent for the past decade, Krystin Clark is a Life Coaching and Counselling graduate of Rhodes Wellness College. A student of metaphysical Universal Law for the past twenty years, Krystin is an ordained metaphysical minister and member of the Canadian International Metaphysical Ministry. Founder of the Kaleidoscope Centre for Soulful Shifts- inspiring mindfulness and gratitude.

Connect with Krystin Clark and view her Spirit Spoons at: www.krystinclark.ca

Bring the Grateful Jar Project entries to life, visit Instagram and search: #thegratefuljarproject